To Caleb and Felix. Always go hard in the paint, fellas—GS

For my cousins. Especially Kordaryl Thomas,
the biggest basketball fan ever—BW

PENGUIN WORKSHOP
An imprint of Penguin Random House LLC, New York

First published in the United States of America by Penguin Workshop,
an imprint of Penguin Random House LLC, New York, 2022

Visit us online at penguinrandomhouse.com.

Library of Congress Cataloging-in-Publication Data is available.

Manufactured in China

ISBN 9780593385913 (pbk)   10 9 8 7 6 5 4 3 2 1
ISBN 9780593385920 (hc)   10 9 8 7 6 5 4 3 2

Lettering by Comicraft
Design by Mary Claire Cruz

This is a work of nonfiction. All of the events that unfold in the narrative
are rooted in historical fact. Some dialogue and characters have been fictionalized
in order to illustrate or teach a historical point.

For more information about your favorite historical figures, places, and events,
please visit whohq.com.

A WHO HQ GRAPHIC NOVEL

Who Is the Man in the Air?

MICHAEL JORDAN

by Gabe Soria
illustrated by Brittney Williams

Penguin Workshop

Introduction

It's the summer of 1997, and American professional basketball team the Chicago Bulls are once again competing for the highest prize in basketball: the National Basketball Association (NBA) Finals championship. The Chicago Bulls are a team to be feared and respected—they are the defending champions of the NBA, and this year they are playing against the Utah Jazz to keep the title. The winner of four out of seven games will determine which team takes the ultimate honor, and right now, the Jazz and the Bulls are tied at two games each. The fifth game in the series is coming up, and the pressure is on the Bulls to win again. But the Bulls have a not-so-secret weapon on their side: team leader and shooting guard Michael Jordan.

Jordan has long been considered one of basketball's greatest players, from his beginning as a junior varsity player in high school to winning a championship with the University of North Carolina Tar Heels in college. Now, at the end of his twelfth season with the Bulls, he has a chance to win his fifth NBA championship with the team. What's more, Jordan is a star on and off the court: He has a signature athletic shoe, Air Jordans, with sportswear brand Nike and starred in the blockbuster movie *Space Jam* just a year prior.

The day of the fifth game in the heated competition has arrived, and everyone is buzzing with adrenaline. If the Bulls win this series, it will be their fifth title in six years. If the Jazz win, it will be their first-ever championship. But the Chicago Bulls have one very big problem: Michael Jordan isn't feeling so good.

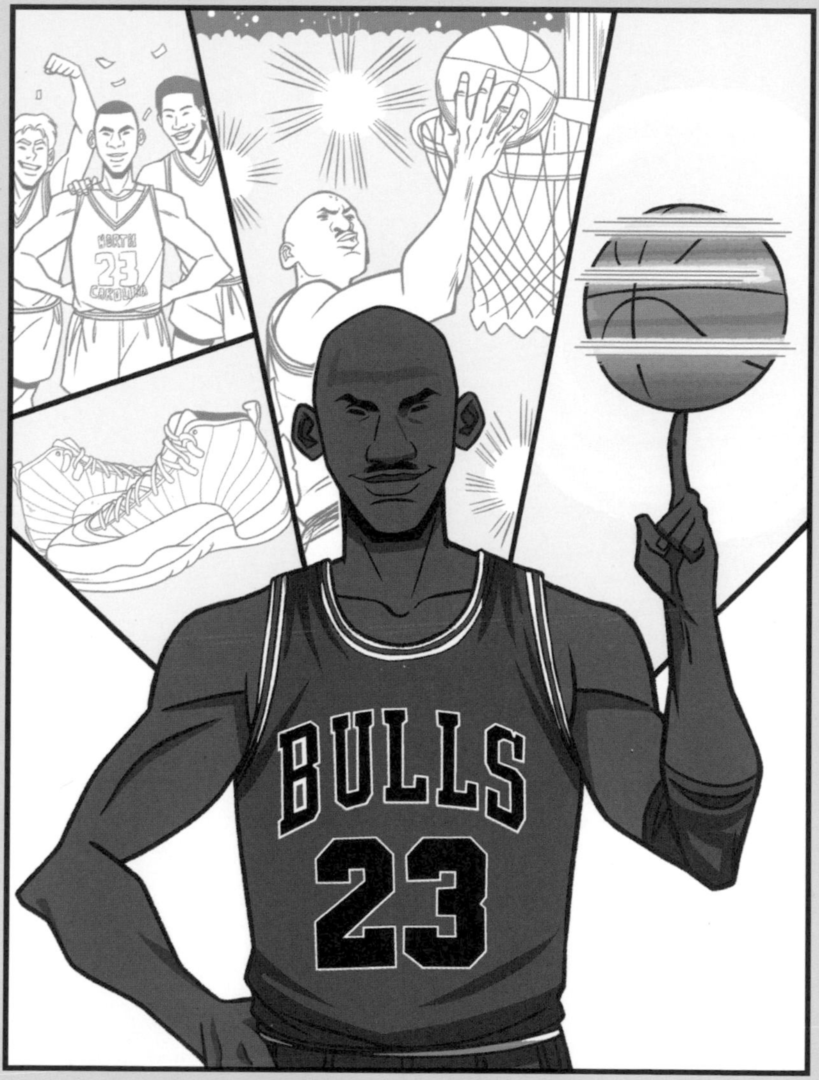
NORTH
23
CAROLINA
BULLS
23

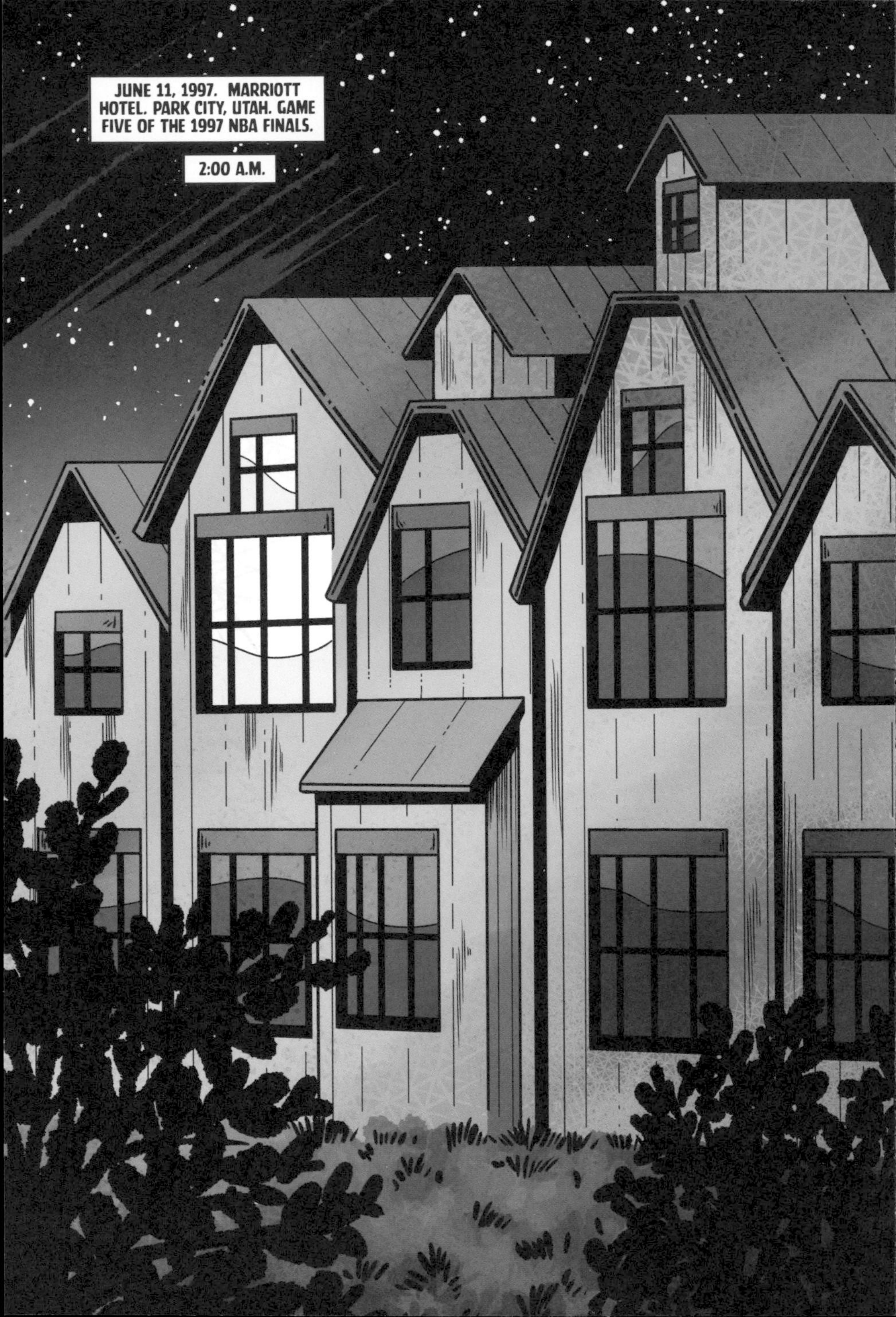
JUNE 11, 1997. MARRIOTT HOTEL. PARK CITY, UTAH. GAME FIVE OF THE 1997 NBA FINALS.
2:00 A.M.

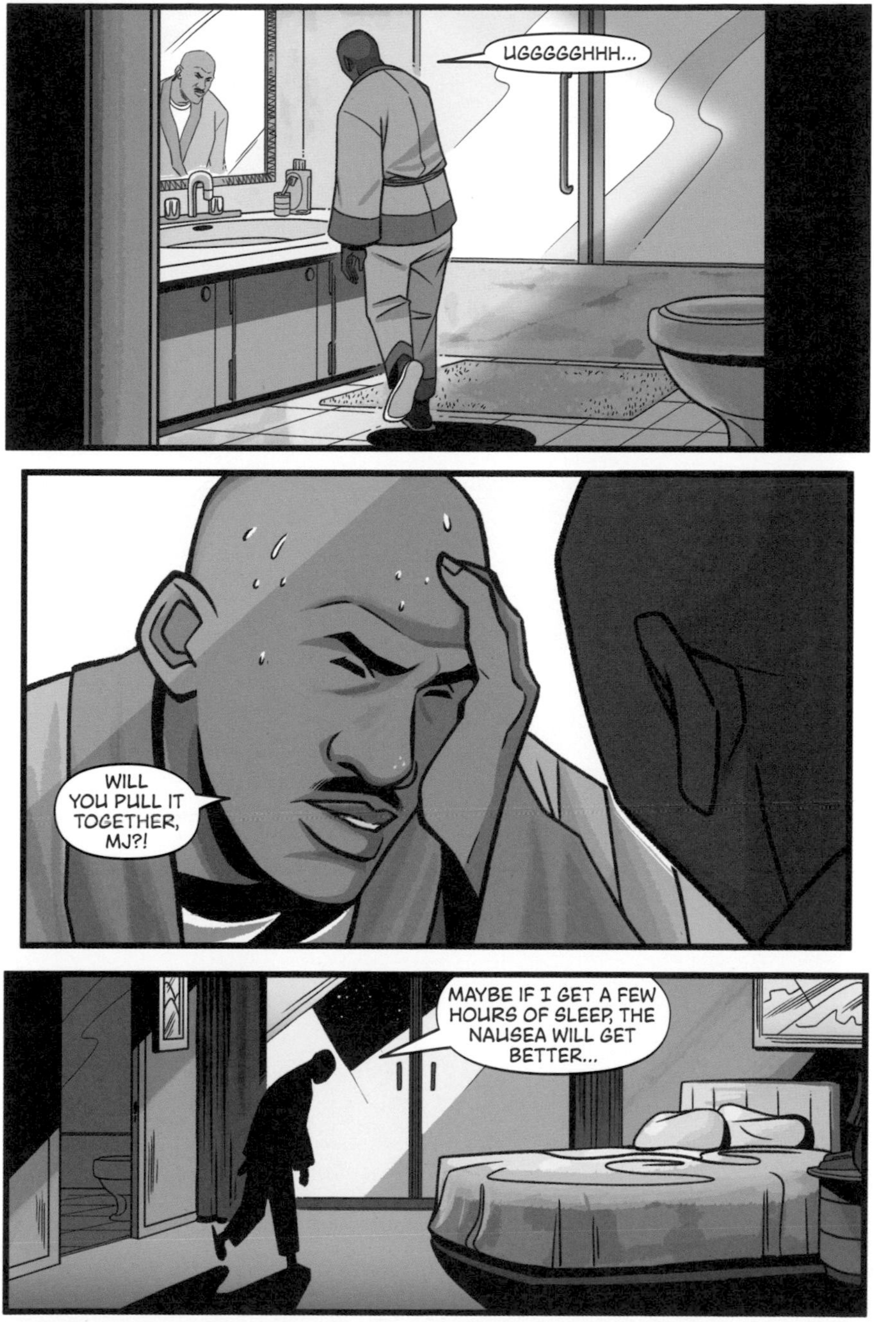
UGGGGGHHH...
WILL YOU PULL IT TOGETHER, MJ?!
MAYBE IF I GET A FEW HOURS OF SLEEP, THE NAUSEA WILL GET BETTER...

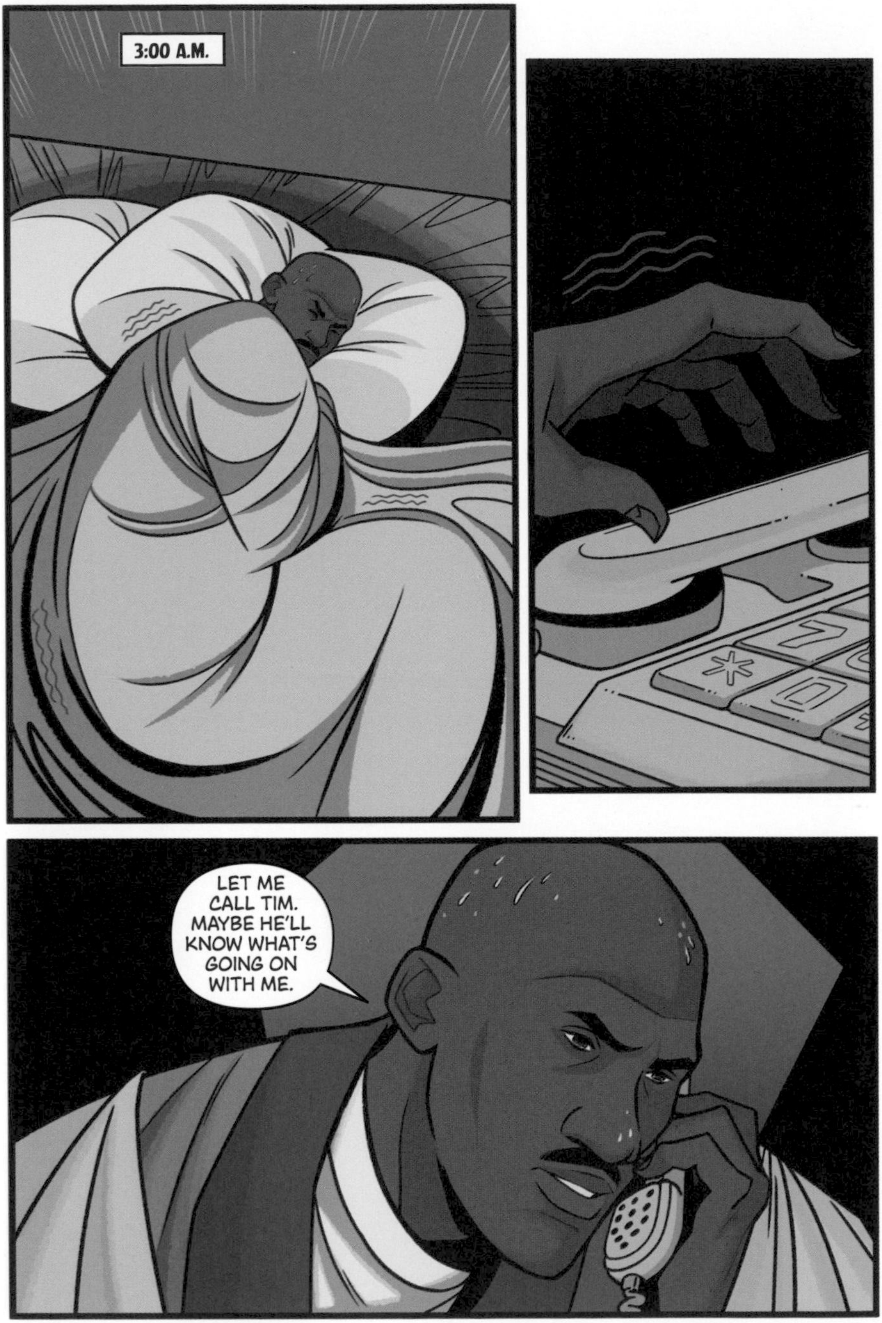
3:00 A.M.
LET ME CALL TIM. MAYBE HE'LL KNOW WHAT'S GOING ON WITH ME.

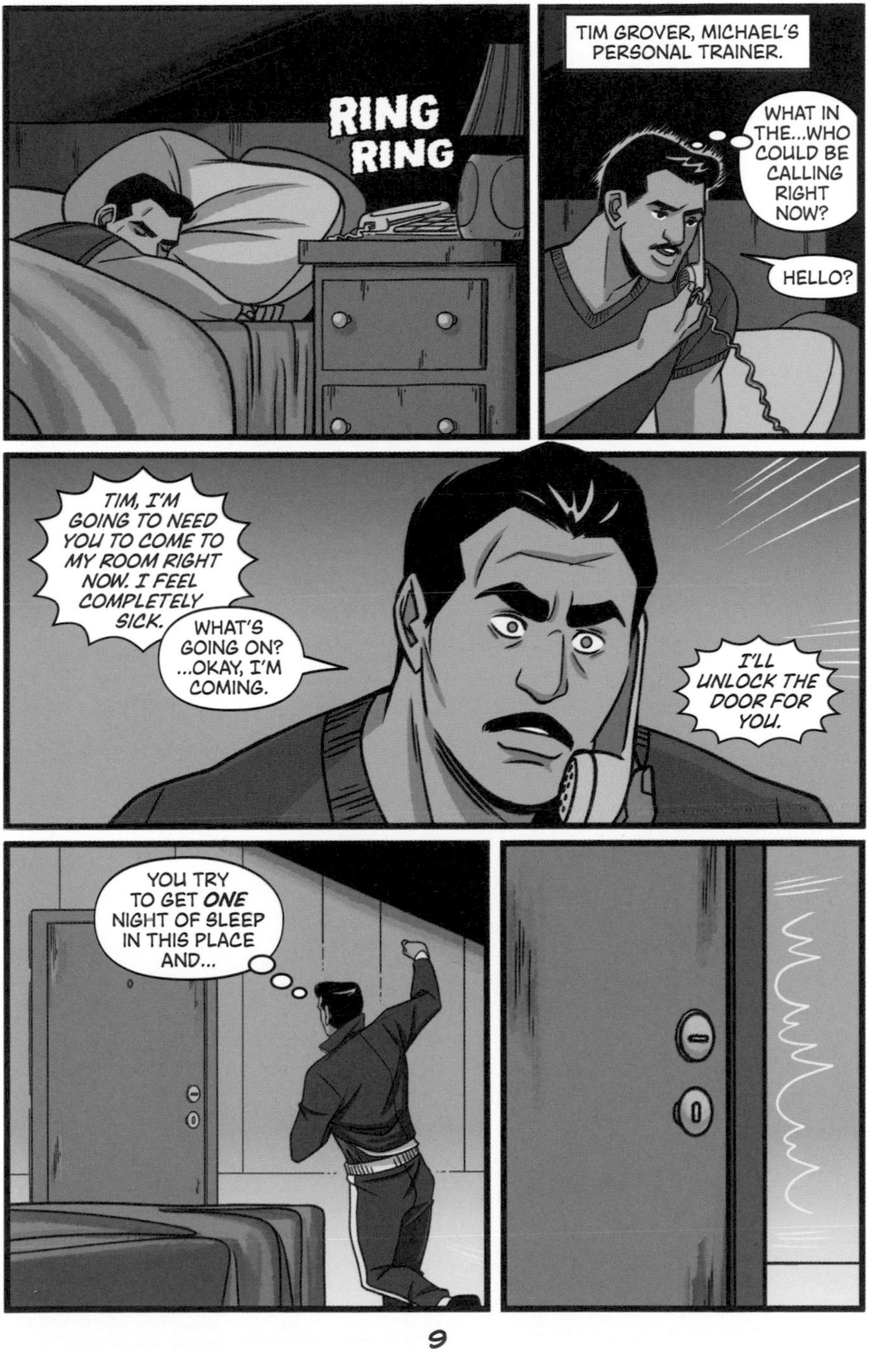
RING
RING
TIM GROVER, MICHAEL'S PERSONAL TRAINER.
WHAT IN THE...WHO COULD BE CALLING RIGHT NOW?
HELLO?
TIM, I'M GOING TO NEED YOU TO COME TO MY ROOM RIGHT NOW. I FEEL COMPLETELY SICK.
WHAT'S GOING ON? ...OKAY, I'M COMING.
I'LL UNLOCK THE DOOR FOR YOU.
YOU TRY TO GET ***ONE*** NIGHT OF SLEEP IN THIS PLACE AND...

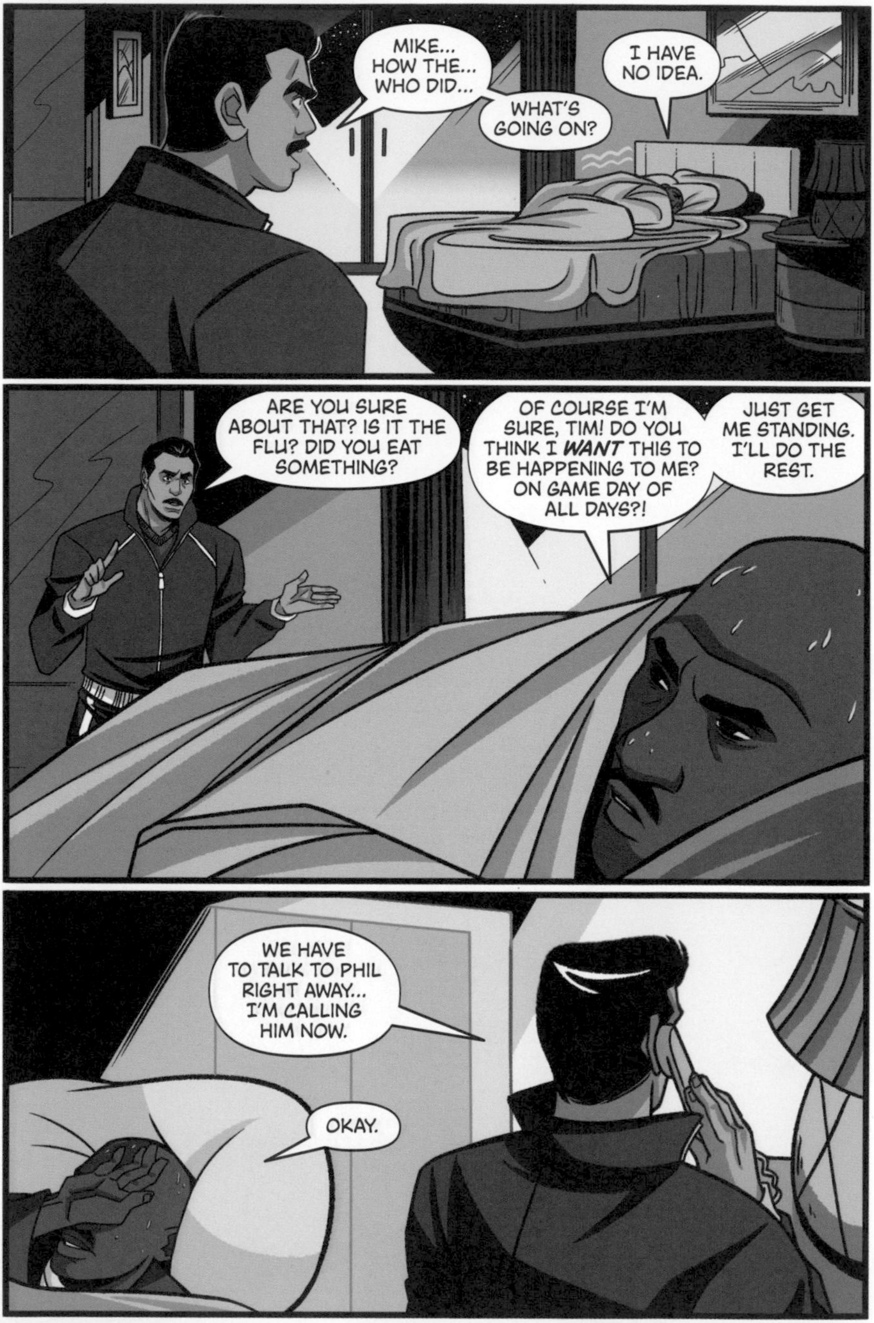
MIKE... HOW THE... WHO DID...
WHAT'S GOING ON?
I HAVE NO IDEA.
ARE YOU SURE ABOUT THAT? IS IT THE FLU? DID YOU EAT SOMETHING?
OF COURSE I'M SURE, TIM! DO YOU THINK I ***WANT*** THIS TO BE HAPPENING TO ME? ON GAME DAY OF ALL DAYS?!
JUST GET ME STANDING. I'LL DO THE REST.
WE HAVE TO TALK TO PHIL RIGHT AWAY... I'M CALLING HIM NOW.
OKAY.

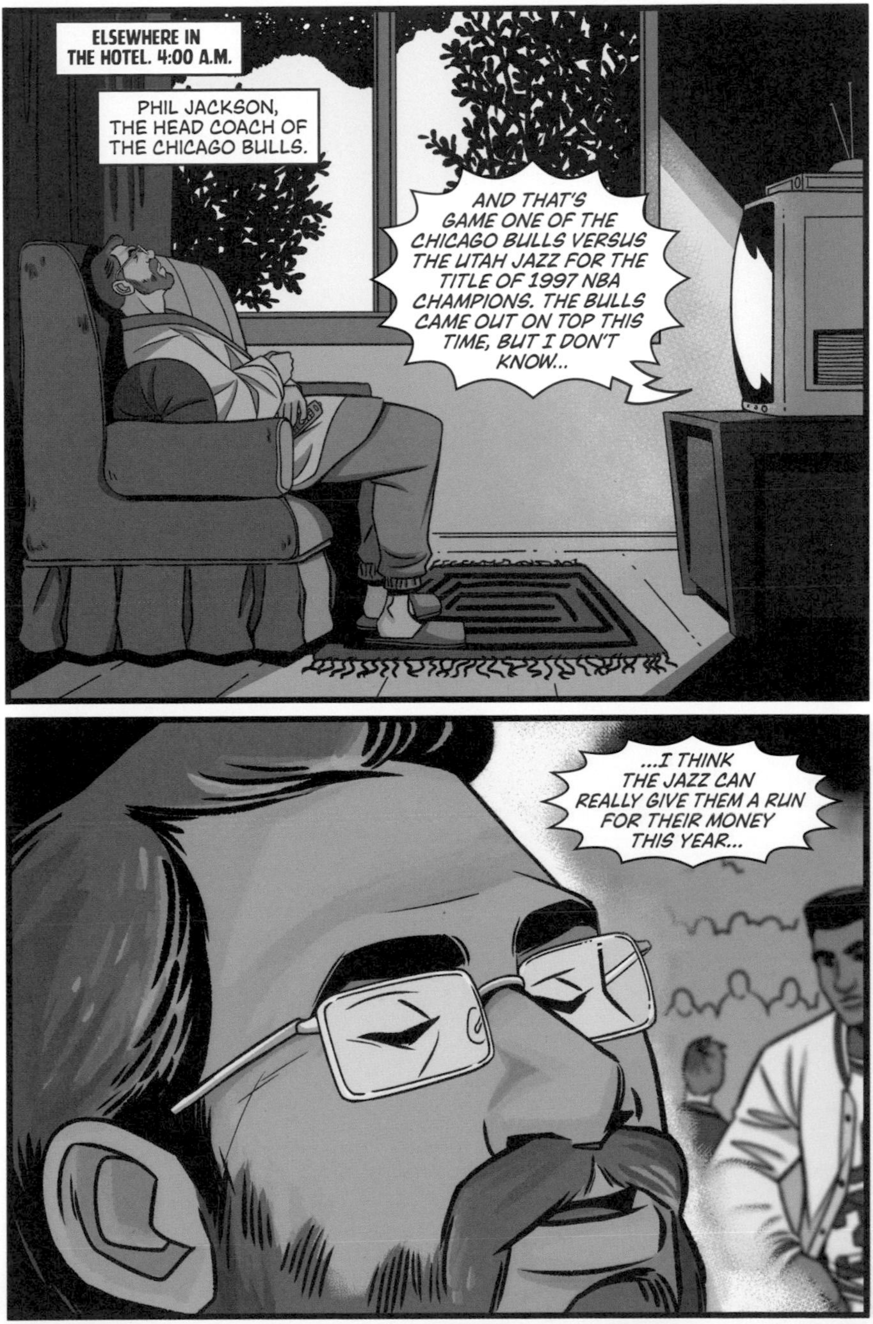
ELSEWHERE IN THE HOTEL. 4:00 A.M.
PHIL JACKSON, THE HEAD COACH OF THE CHICAGO BULLS.
AND THAT'S GAME ONE OF THE CHICAGO BULLS VERSUS THE UTAH JAZZ FOR THE TITLE OF 1997 NBA CHAMPIONS. THE BULLS CAME OUT ON TOP THIS TIME, BUT I DON'T KNOW...
...I THINK THE JAZZ CAN REALLY GIVE THEM A RUN FOR THEIR MONEY THIS YEAR...

GAME ONE! JUNE 1, 1997, UNITED CENTER, CHICAGO.

WELL, AS YOU'VE HEARD IN THE INTRODUCTION OF THE LINEUP, SCOTTIE PIPPEN, WHO WAS A QUESTION MARK, IS IN THE CHICAGO STARTING FIVE. STILL FEELING PAIN FROM THE SOFT-TISSUE INJURY ON THE BOTTOM OF HIS LEFT FOOT, BUT HE WILL GIVE IT A SHOT...

LET'S KEEP AN EYE ON MICHAEL JORDAN—WILL HE SHAKE HANDS WITH KARL MALONE?

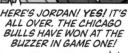

Bulls 84 Jazz 82
1   0

HERE'S JORDAN! YES! IT'S ALL OVER. THE CHICAGO BULLS HAVE WON AT THE BUZZER IN GAME ONE!

GAME TWO! JUNE 4, 1997, UNITED CENTER, CHICAGO.

UTAH JAZZ ARE IN TROUBLE...

NBA Final
CHICAGO BULLS 97
vs
UTAH JAZZ 85

THAT WAS A THREE FROM DENNIS RODMAN IN THE FINAL SECONDS!! THE CHICAGO BULLS HAVE DEFEATED THE UTAH JAZZ, 97–85.

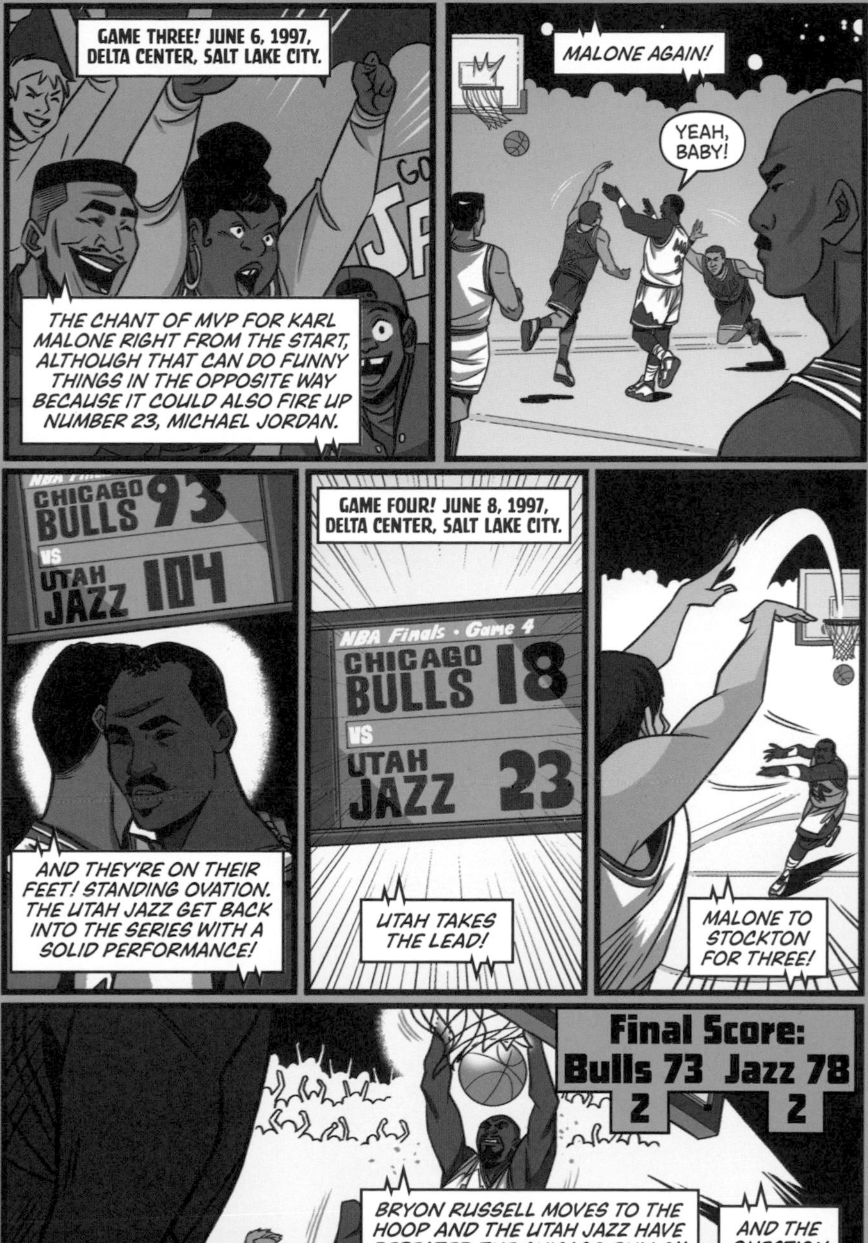
GAME THREE! JUNE 6, 1997, DELTA CENTER, SALT LAKE CITY.
THE CHANT OF MVP FOR KARL MALONE RIGHT FROM THE START, ALTHOUGH THAT CAN DO FUNNY THINGS IN THE OPPOSITE WAY BECAUSE IT COULD ALSO FIRE UP NUMBER 23, MICHAEL JORDAN.
MALONE AGAIN!
YEAH, BABY!
CHICAGO BULLS 93
VS
UTAH JAZZ 104
AND THEY'RE ON THEIR FEET! STANDING OVATION. THE UTAH JAZZ GET BACK INTO THE SERIES WITH A SOLID PERFORMANCE!
GAME FOUR! JUNE 8, 1997, DELTA CENTER, SALT LAKE CITY.
NBA Finals • Game 4
CHICAGO BULLS 18
VS
UTAH JAZZ 23
UTAH TAKES THE LEAD!
MALONE TO STOCKTON FOR THREE!
Final Score:
Bulls 73 Jazz 78
2 2
BRYON RUSSELL MOVES TO THE HOOP AND THE UTAH JAZZ HAVE DEFEATED THE CHICAGO BULLS!! THE SERIES IS TIED AT TWO!!
AND THE QUESTION IS THIS...

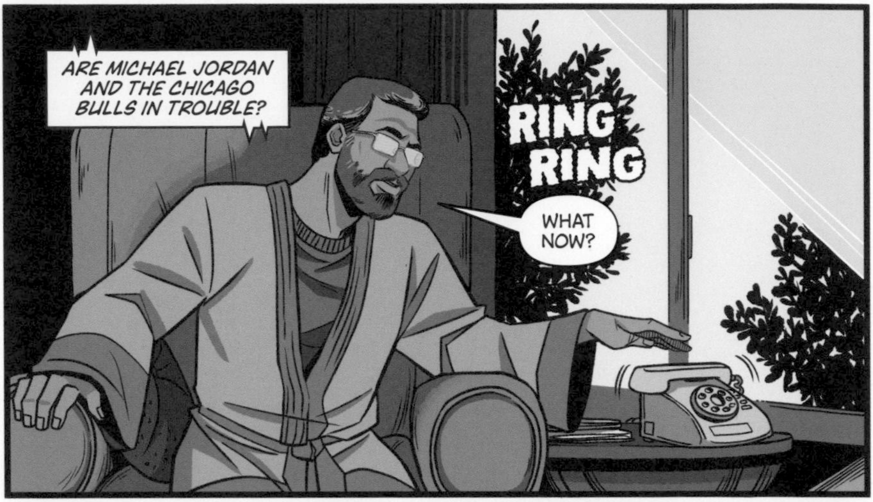
ARE MICHAEL JORDAN AND THE CHICAGO BULLS IN TROUBLE?
RING RING
WHAT NOW?

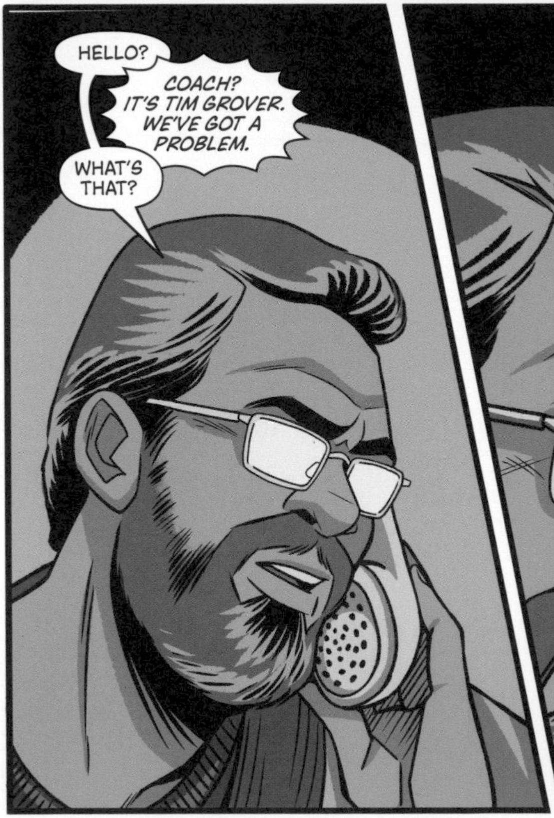
HELLO?
COACH? IT'S TIM GROVER. WE'VE GOT A PROBLEM.
WHAT'S THAT?

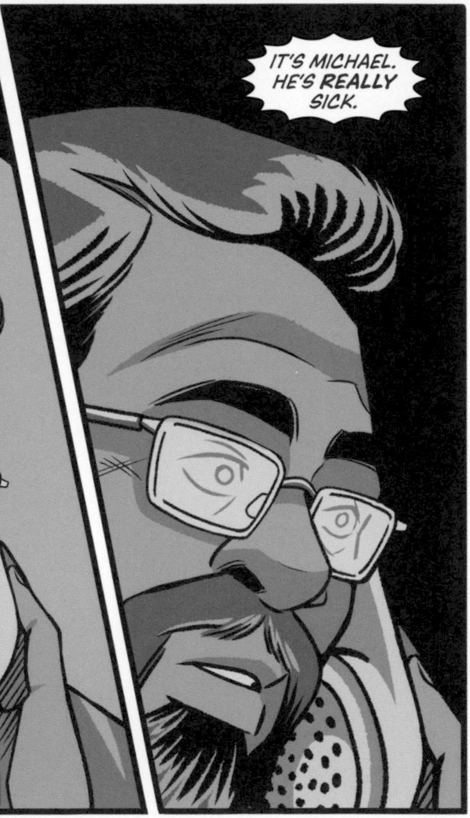
IT'S MICHAEL. HE'S REALLY SICK.

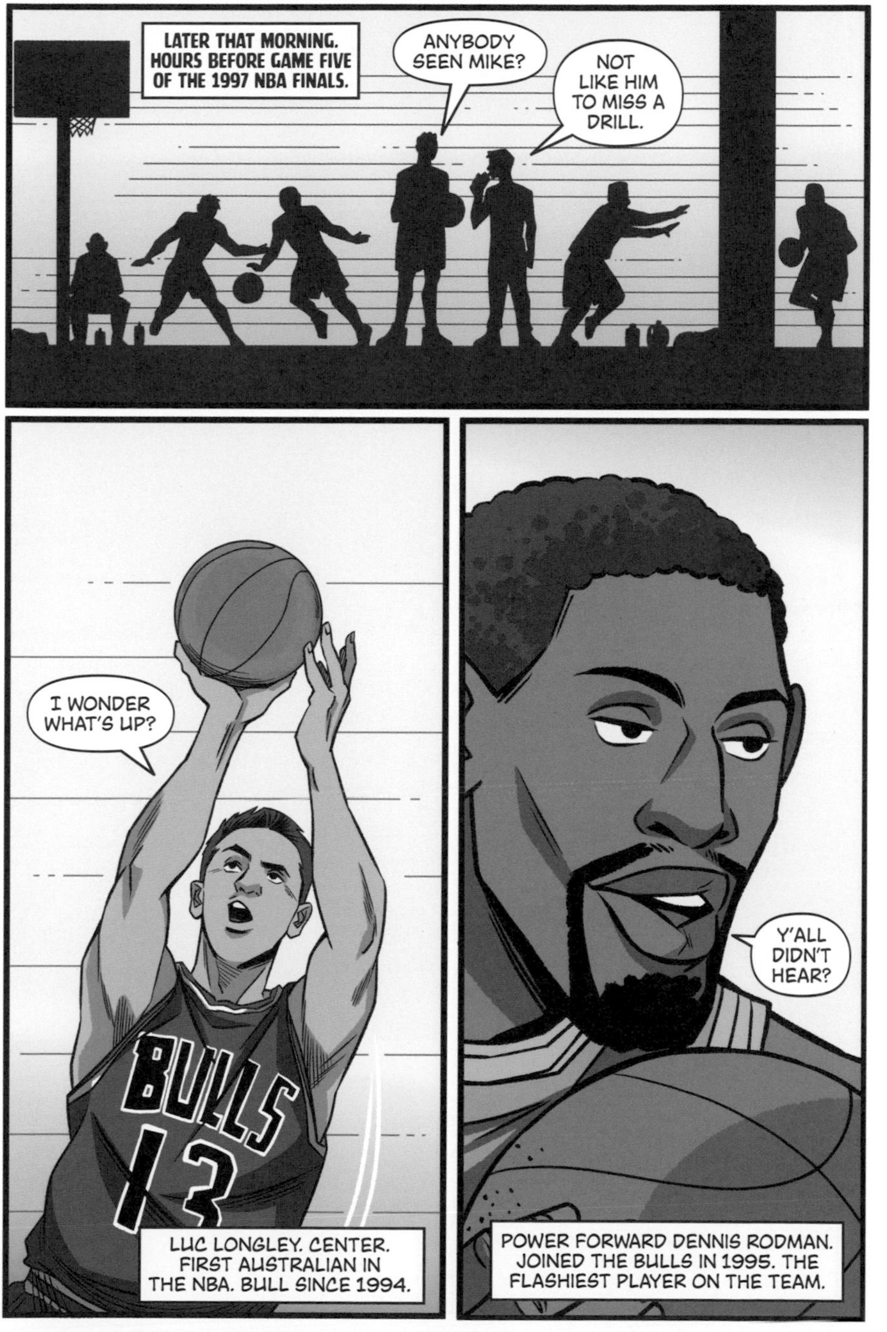
LATER THAT MORNING. HOURS BEFORE GAME FIVE OF THE 1997 NBA FINALS.
ANYBODY SEEN MIKE?
NOT LIKE HIM TO MISS A DRILL.
I WONDER WHAT'S UP?
BULLS 13
LUC LONGLEY. CENTER. FIRST AUSTRALIAN IN THE NBA. BULL SINCE 1994.
Y'ALL DIDN'T HEAR?
POWER FORWARD DENNIS RODMAN. JOINED THE BULLS IN 1995. THE FLASHIEST PLAYER ON THE TEAM.

Positions in Basketball

A professional basketball game is played in four twelve-minute quarters and divided into two halves. The games are played with five people on each team on the court. The positions are the power forward, the center, the point guard, the small forward, and the shooting guard, each with their own important role to play. THE CENTER is the focus of a lot of the action; centers are sometimes the biggest player on the team, and they use their size to get close to the basket and score. THE POINT GUARD focuses on defense against the other team, and their main job is to stop them from scoring. THE POWER FORWARD plays a role much like the center, focusing on offense, particularly rebounds from the basket after a player takes a shot, and facing off against very tall opponents. THE SMALL FORWARD is a versatile player who can play both offense and defense against players large and small. THE SHOOTING GUARD is the best scorer on the team, specializing in (but not limited to) making baskets from farther away.

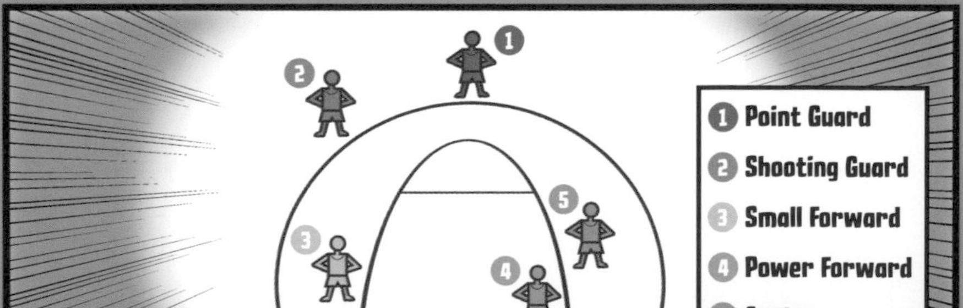

1
2
3
4
5
1 Point Guard
2 Shooting Guard
3 Small Forward
4 Power Forward
5 Center

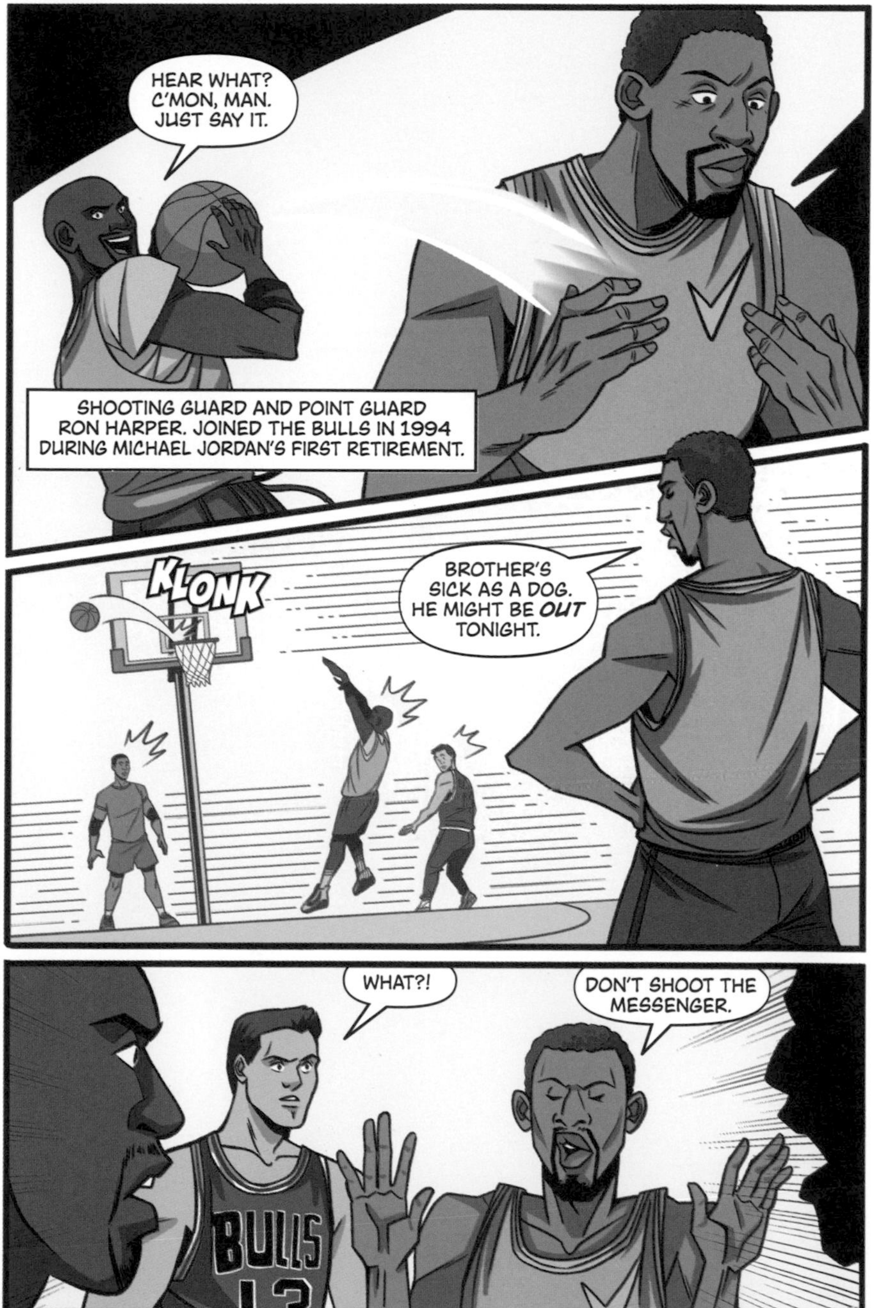
HEAR WHAT? C'MON, MAN. JUST SAY IT.
SHOOTING GUARD AND POINT GUARD RON HARPER. JOINED THE BULLS IN 1994 DURING MICHAEL JORDAN'S FIRST RETIREMENT.
KLONK
BROTHER'S SICK AS A DOG. HE MIGHT BE OUT TONIGHT.
WHAT?!
DON'T SHOOT THE MESSENGER.
BULLS

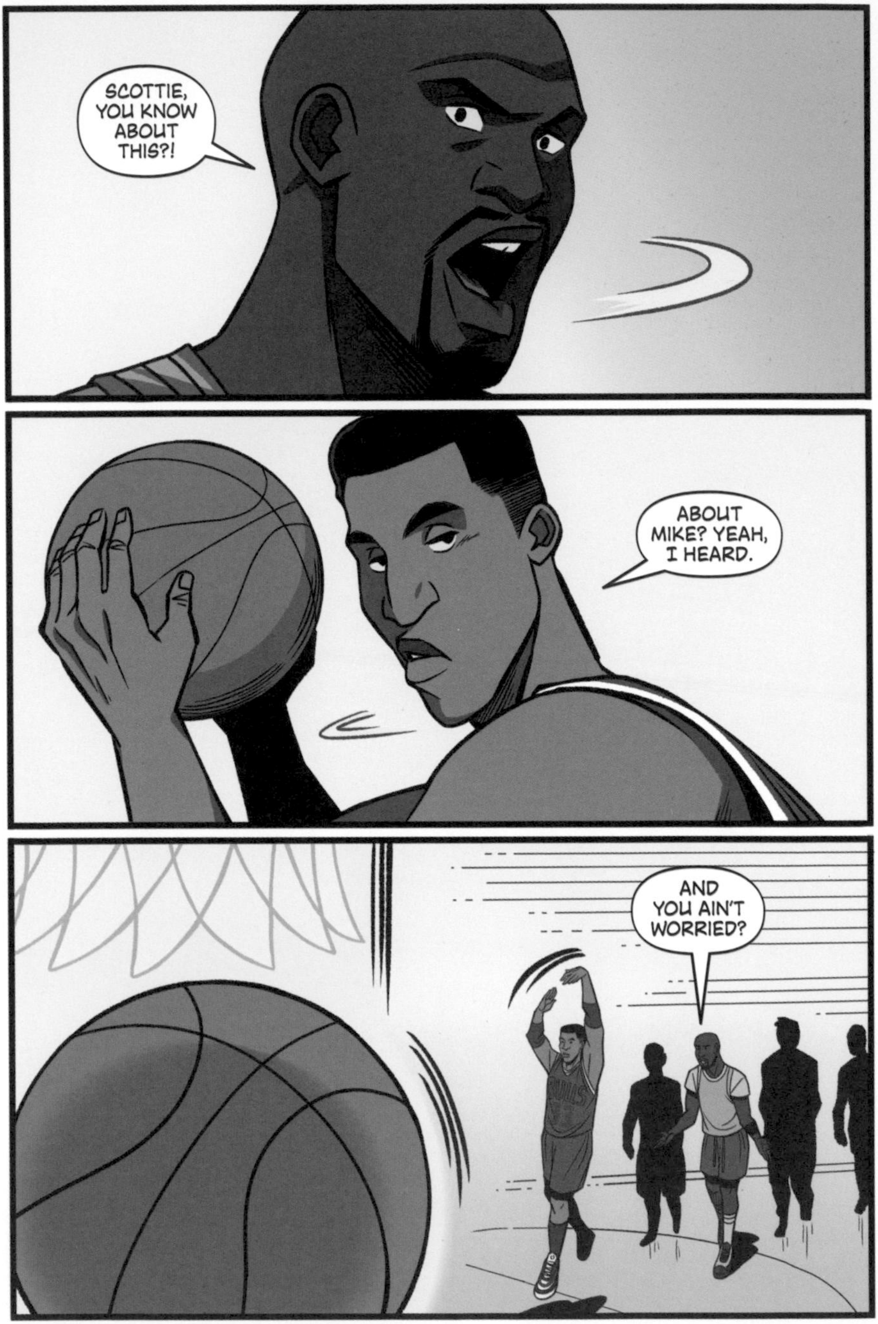
SCOTTIE, YOU KNOW ABOUT THIS?!
ABOUT MIKE? YEAH, I HEARD.
AND YOU AIN'T WORRIED?
BULLS

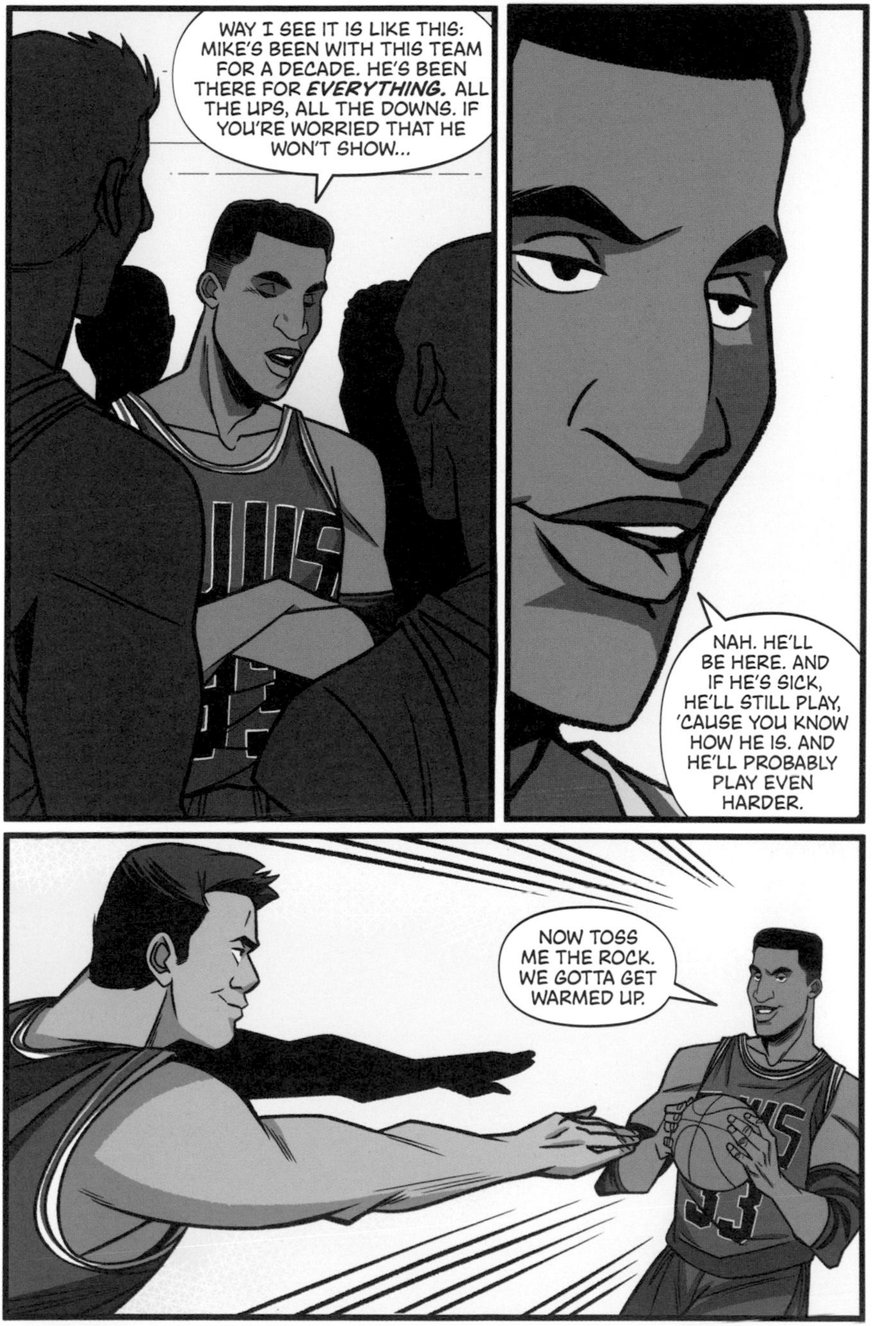
WAY I SEE IT IS LIKE THIS: MIKE'S BEEN WITH THIS TEAM FOR A DECADE. HE'S BEEN THERE FOR *EVERYTHING.* ALL THE UPS, ALL THE DOWNS. IF YOU'RE WORRIED THAT HE WON'T SHOW...
NAH. HE'LL BE HERE. AND IF HE'S SICK, HE'LL STILL PLAY, 'CAUSE YOU KNOW HOW HE IS. AND HE'LL PROBABLY PLAY EVEN HARDER.
NOW TOSS ME THE ROCK. WE GOTTA GET WARMED UP.

Scottie Pippen

Born on September 25, 1965, in Hamburg, Arkansas, Scottie Pippen loved to play football and basketball from an early age. He played basketball all throughout high school, leading his team to the state playoffs and earning top conference honors. But because he stood at just six feet one inch tall and weighed less than 150 pounds at the time, no college offered him a basketball scholarship. Eventually, Scottie was accepted to the University of Central Arkansas and ended up making the team as a walk-on (a player who becomes part of the team without being recruited beforehand). During his time in college, Pippen grew to six foot eight and became a top-level player—as well as a favorite among NBA scouts.

Drafted by the Seattle SuperSonics and traded to the Bulls in 1987, Scottie played the position of small forward alongside Michael Jordan in every one of the team's championship seasons the following decade and was crucial in shaping the unstoppable Bulls dynasty in the 1990s. He was considered to be the other leader of the Bulls, especially after Michael Jordan's first retirement from the team. Pippen also played on the 1992 Summer Olympics "Dream Team" in Barcelona where they won the gold medal.

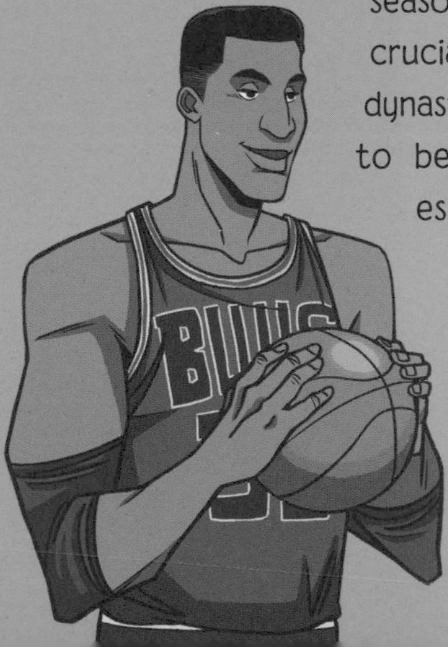

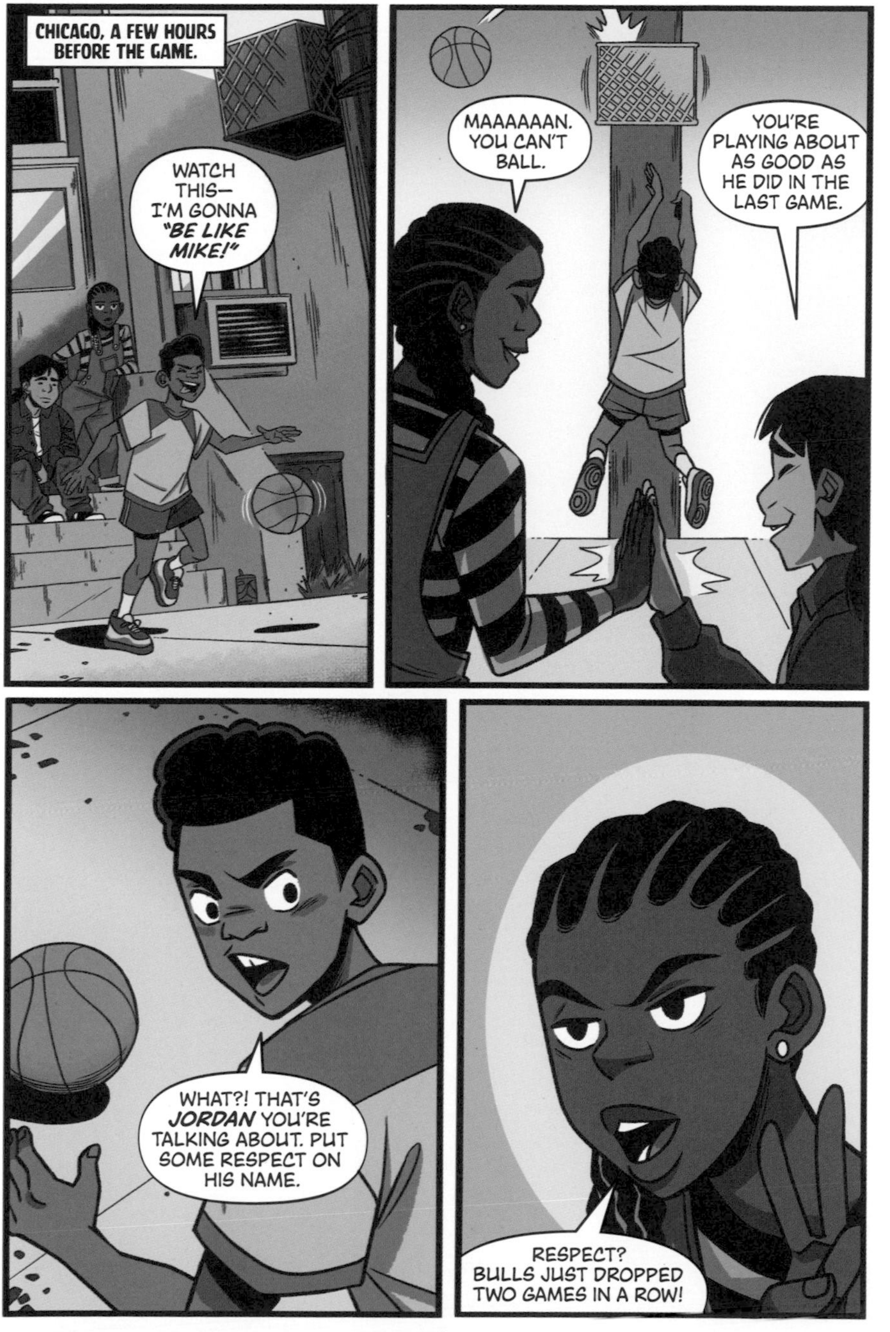
CHICAGO, A FEW HOURS BEFORE THE GAME.
WATCH THIS— I'M GONNA ***"BE LIKE MIKE!"***
MAAAAAAN. YOU CAN'T BALL.
YOU'RE PLAYING ABOUT AS GOOD AS HE DID IN THE LAST GAME.
WHAT?! THAT'S ***JORDAN*** YOU'RE TALKING ABOUT. PUT SOME RESPECT ON HIS NAME.
RESPECT? BULLS JUST DROPPED TWO GAMES IN A ROW!

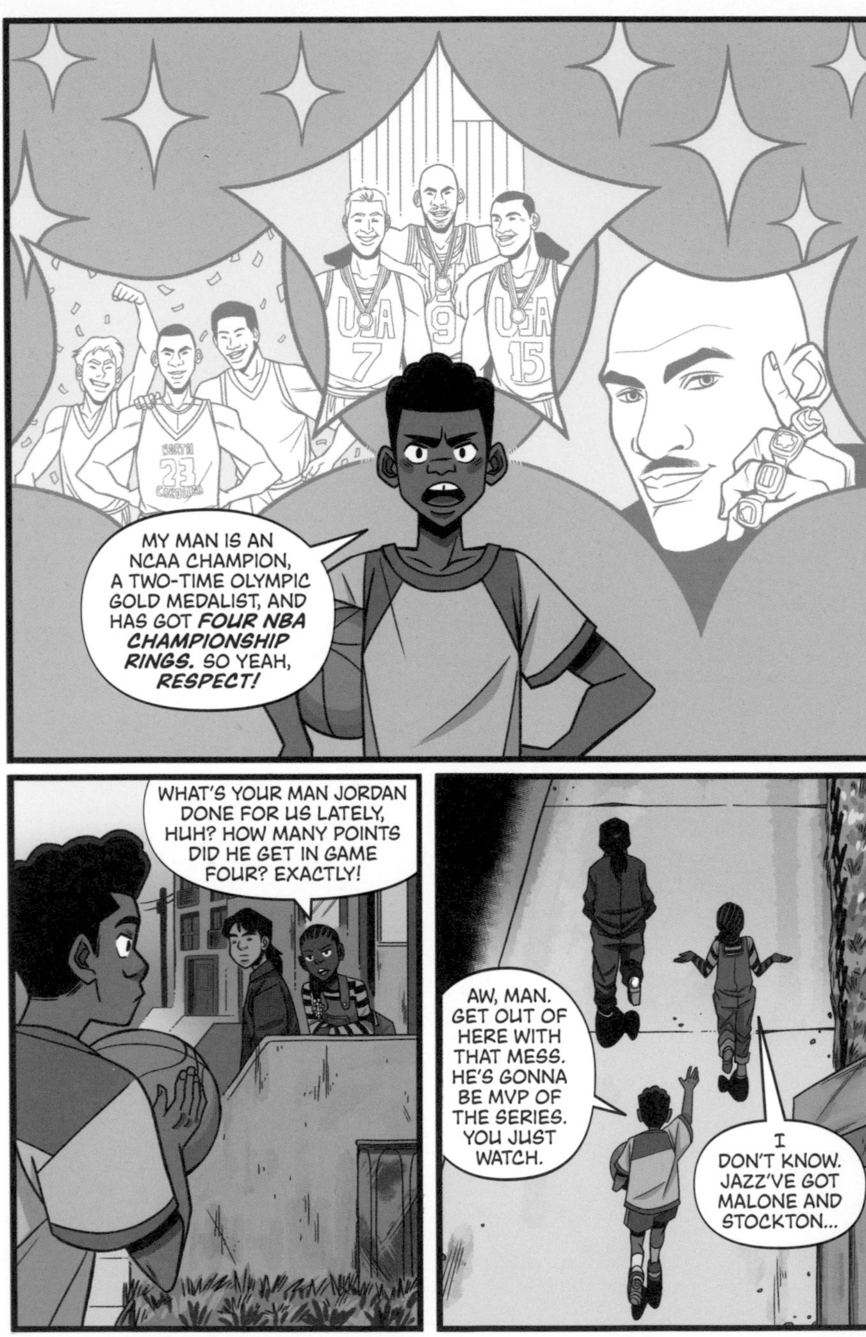
MY MAN IS AN NCAA CHAMPION, A TWO-TIME OLYMPIC GOLD MEDALIST, AND HAS GOT ***FOUR NBA CHAMPIONSHIP RINGS.*** SO YEAH, ***RESPECT!***
WHAT'S YOUR MAN JORDAN DONE FOR US LATELY, HUH? HOW MANY POINTS DID HE GET IN GAME FOUR? EXACTLY!
AW, MAN. GET OUT OF HERE WITH THAT MESS. HE'S GONNA BE MVP OF THE SERIES. YOU JUST WATCH.
I DON'T KNOW. JAZZ'VE GOT MALONE AND STOCKTON...

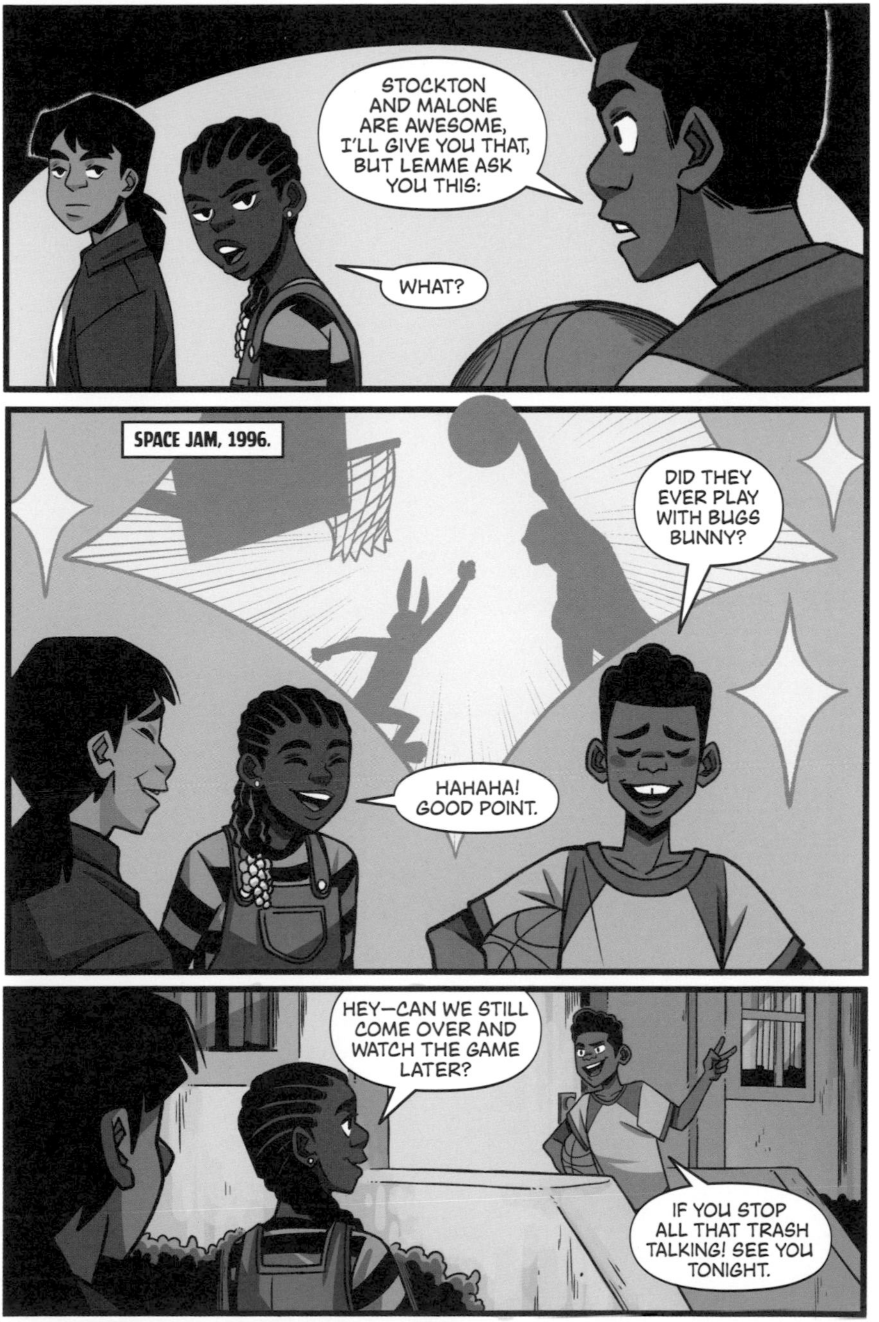
STOCKTON AND MALONE ARE AWESOME, I'LL GIVE YOU THAT, BUT LEMME ASK YOU THIS:
WHAT?
SPACE JAM, 1996.
DID THEY EVER PLAY WITH BUGS BUNNY?
HAHAHA! GOOD POINT.
HEY—CAN WE STILL COME OVER AND WATCH THE GAME LATER?
IF YOU STOP ALL THAT TRASH TALKING! SEE YOU TONIGHT.

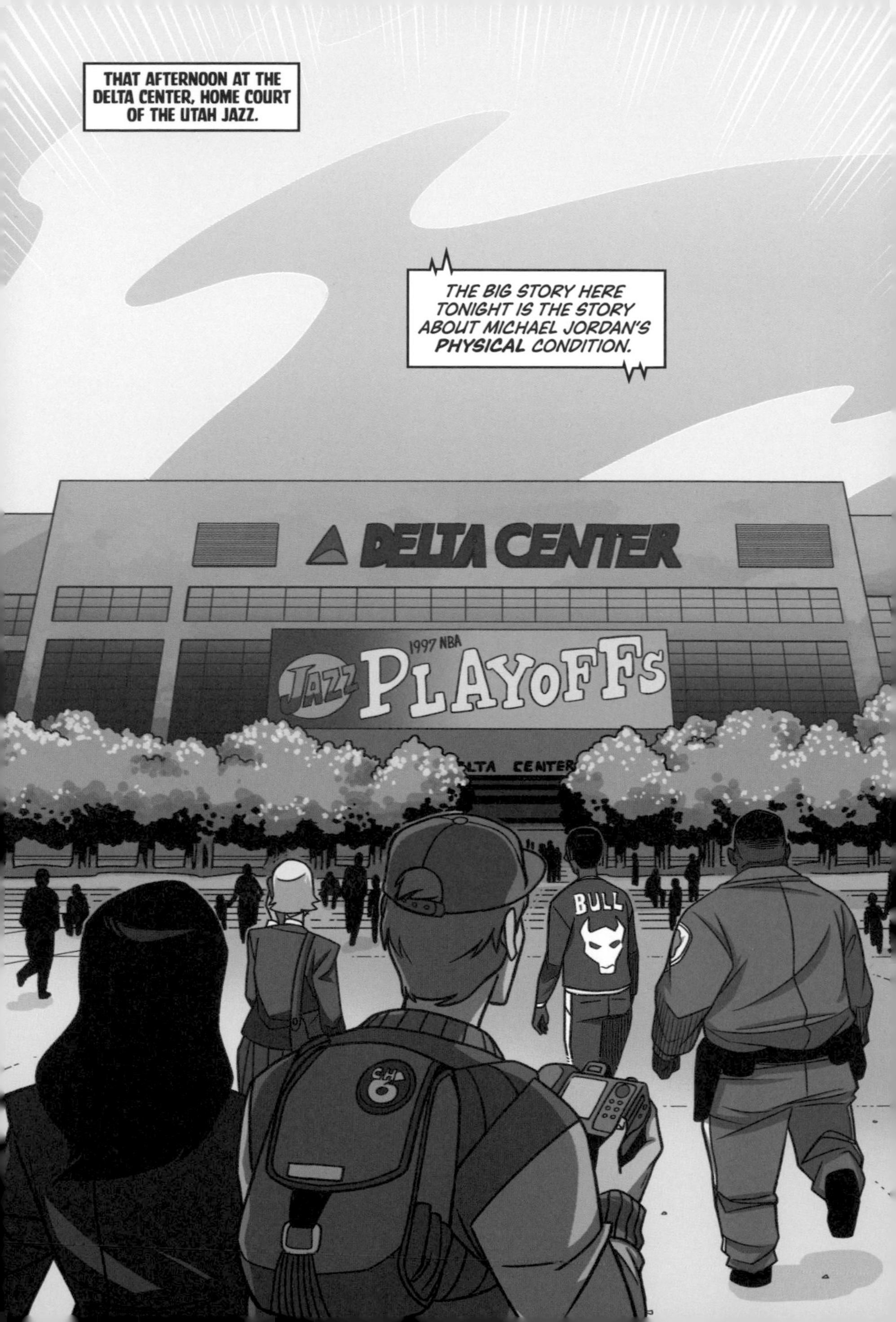
THAT AFTERNOON AT THE DELTA CENTER, HOME COURT OF THE UTAH JAZZ.
THE BIG STORY HERE TONIGHT IS THE STORY ABOUT MICHAEL JORDAN'S PHYSICAL CONDITION.
DELTA CENTER
1997 NBA
JAZZ PLAYOFFS
BULL

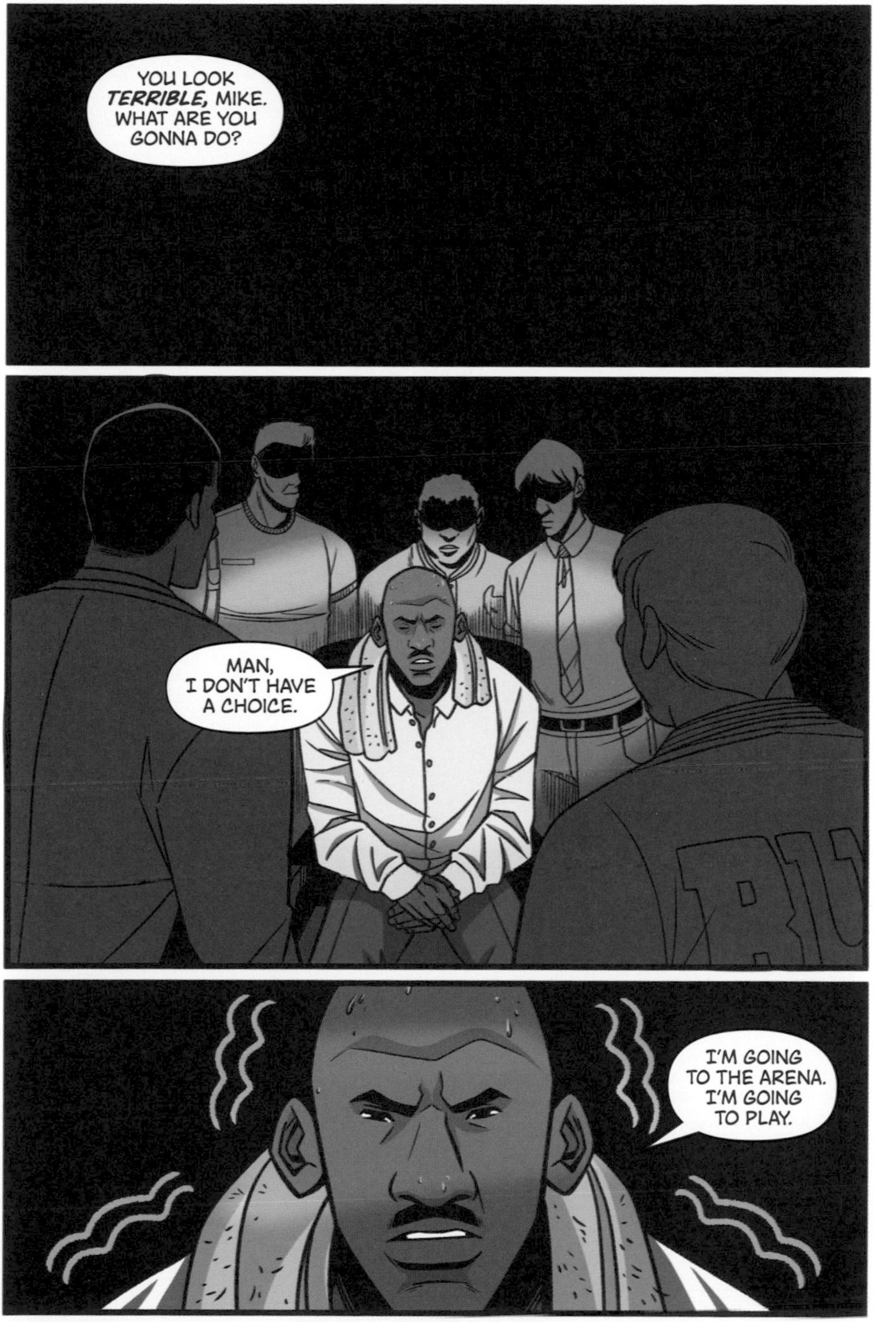
YOU LOOK *TERRIBLE,* MIKE. WHAT ARE YOU GONNA DO?
MAN, I DON'T HAVE A CHOICE.
I'M GOING TO THE ARENA. I'M GOING TO PLAY.

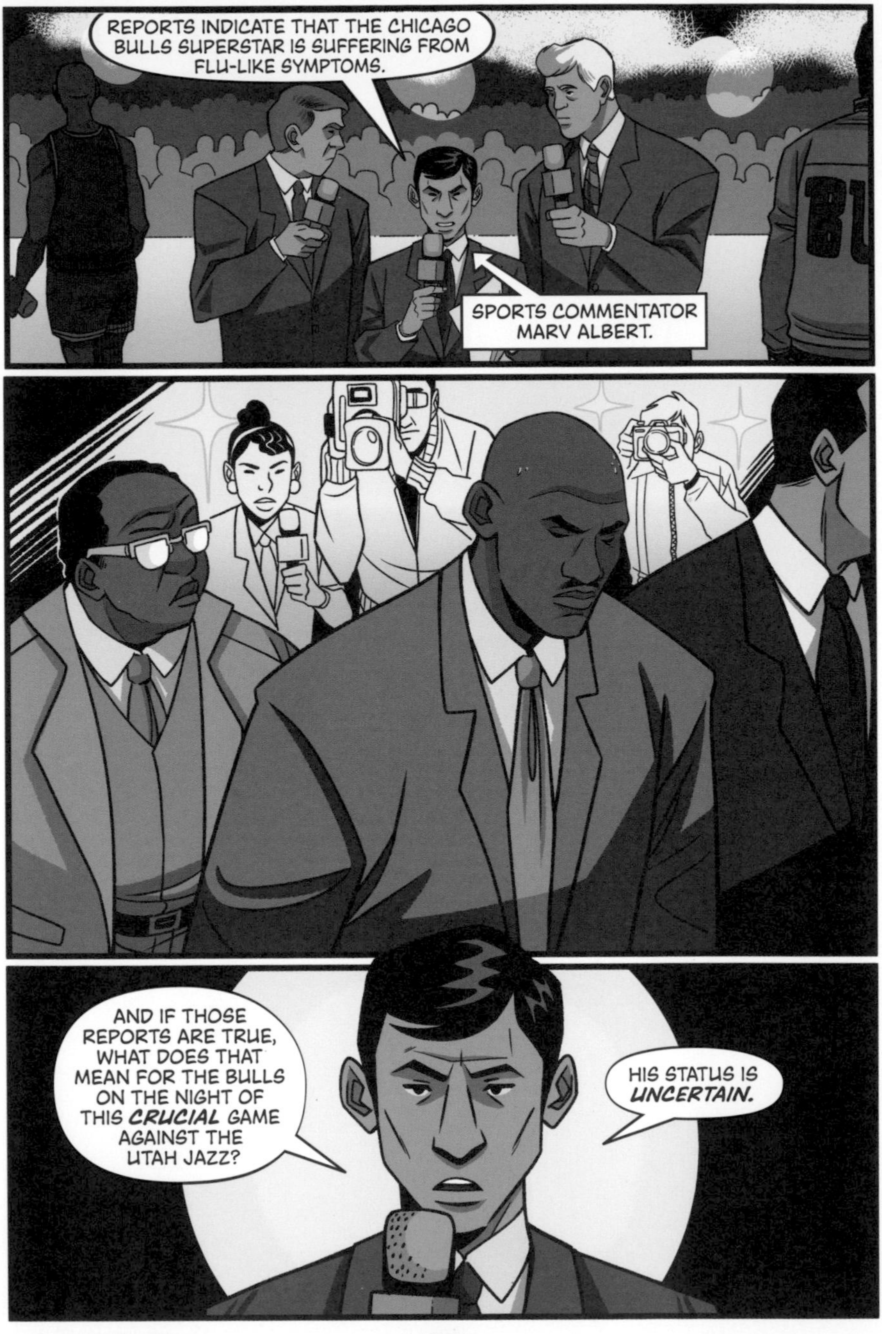
REPORTS INDICATE THAT THE CHICAGO BULLS SUPERSTAR IS SUFFERING FROM FLU-LIKE SYMPTOMS.
SPORTS COMMENTATOR MARV ALBERT.
AND IF THOSE REPORTS ARE TRUE, WHAT DOES THAT MEAN FOR THE BULLS ON THE NIGHT OF THIS *CRUCIAL* GAME AGAINST THE UTAH JAZZ?
HIS STATUS IS *UNCERTAIN.*

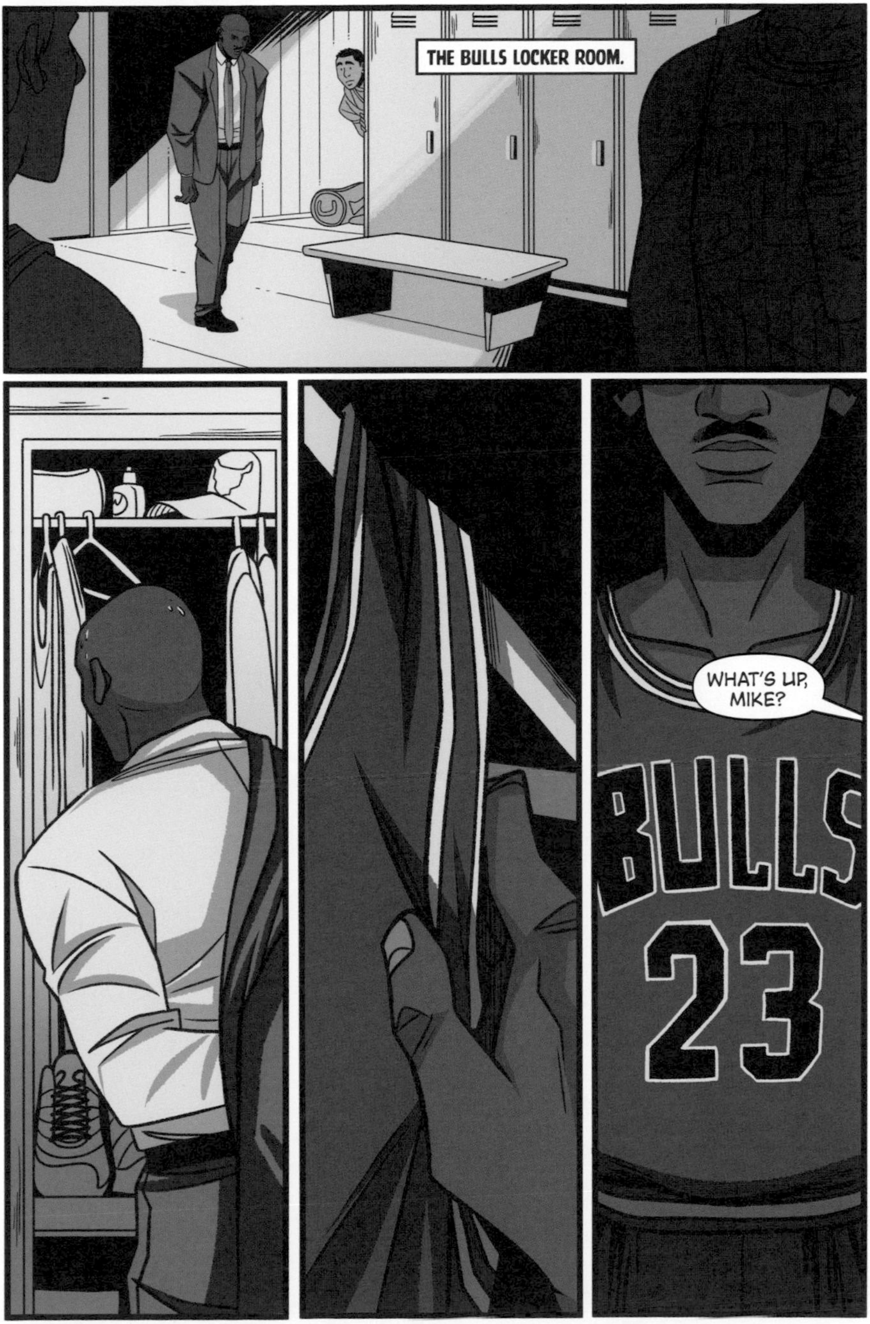
THE BULLS LOCKER ROOM.
WHAT'S UP, MIKE?
BULLS
23

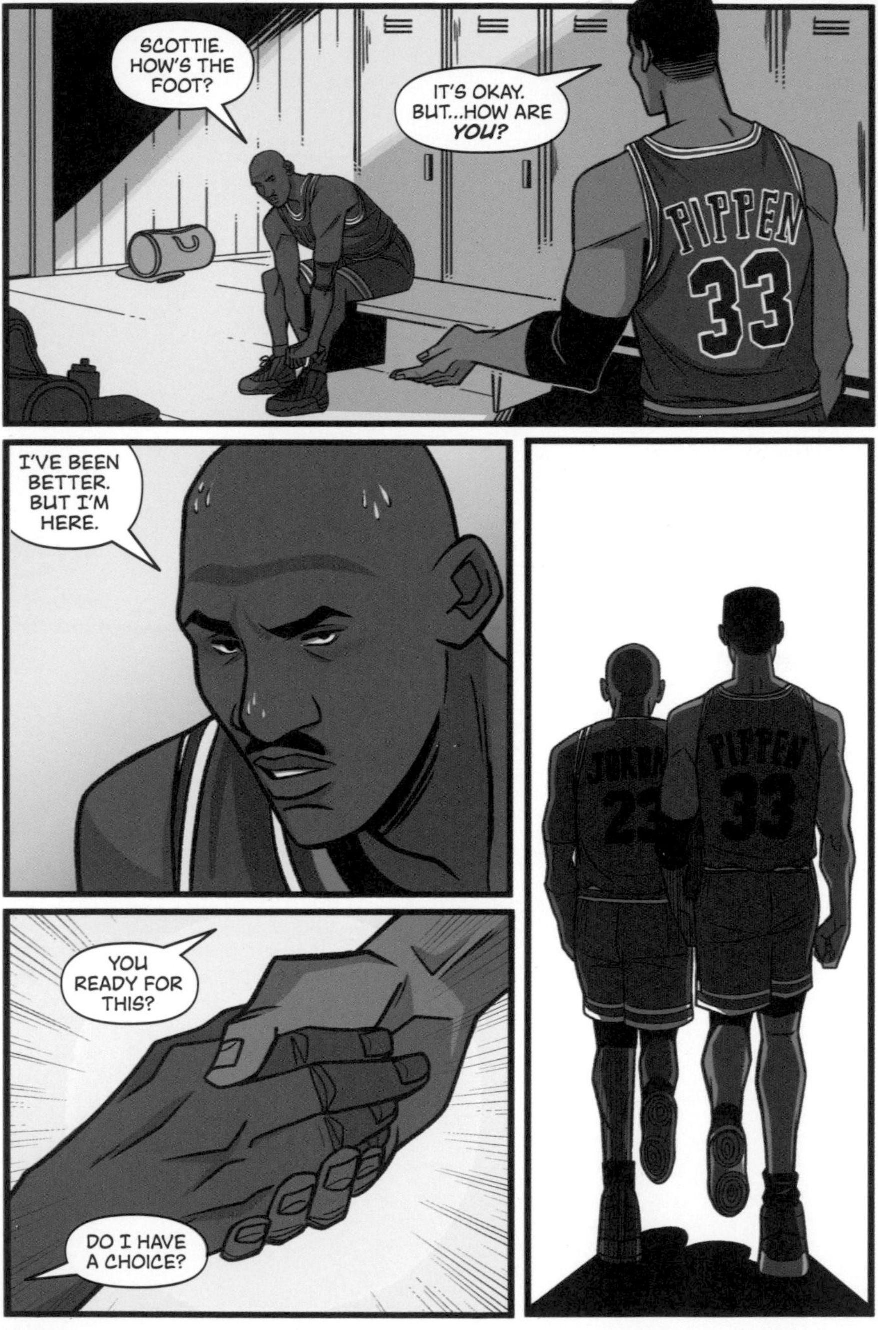
SCOTTIE. HOW'S THE FOOT?
IT'S OKAY. BUT...HOW ARE *YOU?*
PIPPEN 33
I'VE BEEN BETTER. BUT I'M HERE.
YOU READY FOR THIS?
DO I HAVE A CHOICE?
PIPPEN 33

Air Jordan

Athlete-endorsed athletic shoes are almost as old as professional sports itself. There's the Chuck Taylor, or "Chucks," that were made for and named after early semi-pro basketball player Chuck Taylor. There's also the Jack Purcell shoe, which is named after a Canadian badminton player, and many more. But the most groundbreaking and game-changing athlete shoe ever is arguably the Air Jordan, named after Michael Jordan. Designed for Michael's personal use in 1984, the next year, the shoe was first made available to the general public and was an immediate hit, generating massive sales and even some controversy because of how coveted and expensive they were. Today, the shoes known to many simply as "Jordans" continue to be one of the most popular athletic shoes around.

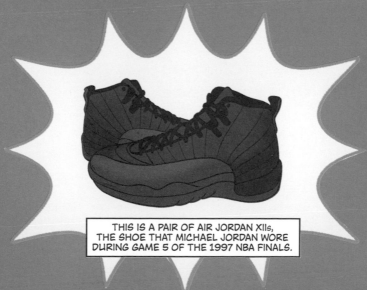

THIS IS A PAIR OF AIR JORDAN XIIs,
THE SHOE THAT MICHAEL JORDAN WORE
DURING GAME 5 OF THE 1997 NBA FINALS.

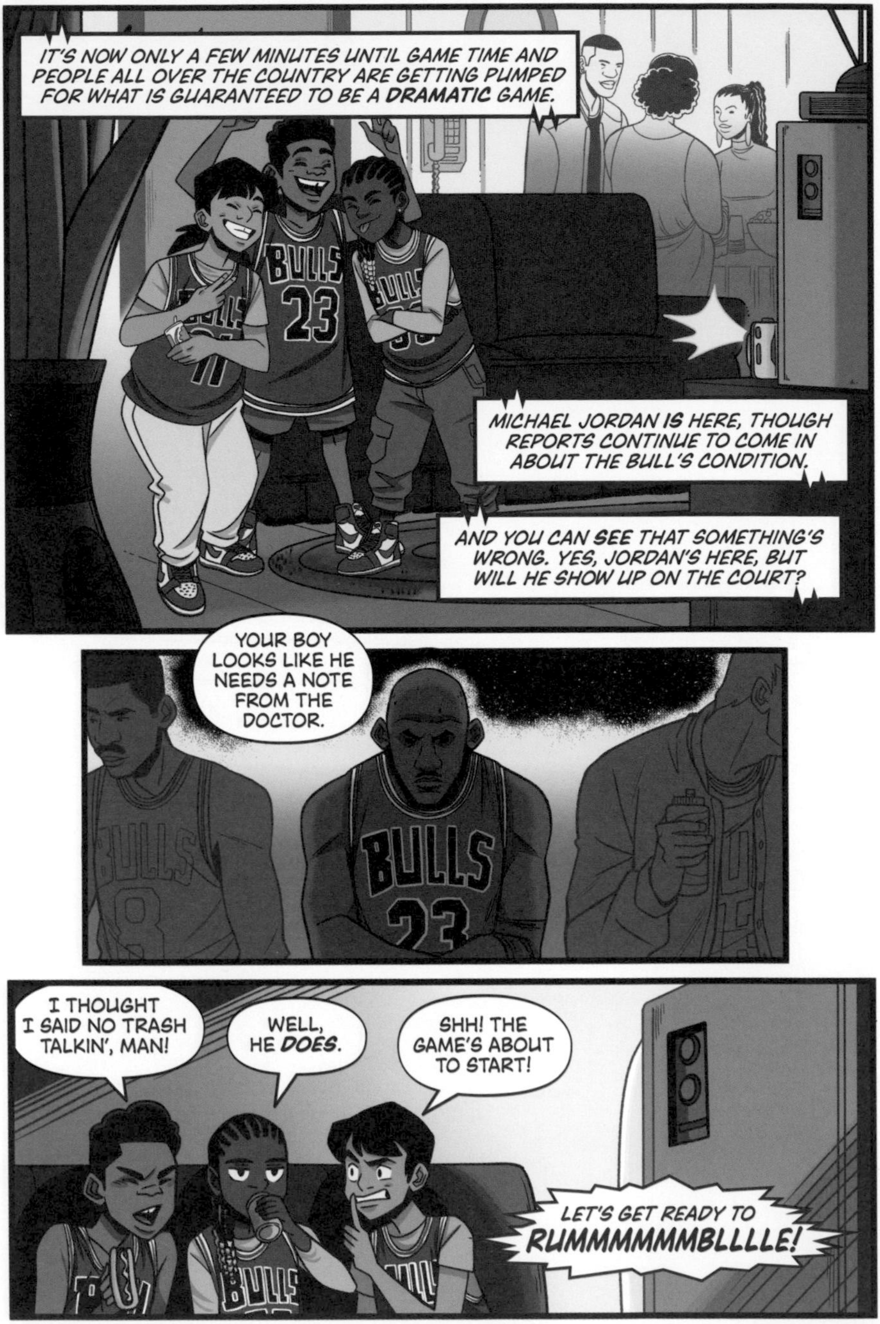
IT'S NOW ONLY A FEW MINUTES UNTIL GAME TIME AND PEOPLE ALL OVER THE COUNTRY ARE GETTING PUMPED FOR WHAT IS GUARANTEED TO BE A **DRAMATIC** GAME.
MICHAEL JORDAN **IS** HERE, THOUGH REPORTS CONTINUE TO COME IN ABOUT THE BULL'S CONDITION.
AND YOU CAN **SEE** THAT SOMETHING'S WRONG. YES, JORDAN'S HERE, BUT WILL HE SHOW UP ON THE COURT?
YOUR BOY LOOKS LIKE HE NEEDS A NOTE FROM THE DOCTOR.
I THOUGHT I SAID NO TRASH TALKIN', MAN!
WELL, HE ***DOES***.
SHH! THE GAME'S ABOUT TO START!
LET'S GET READY TO **RUMMMMMMBLLLLE!**

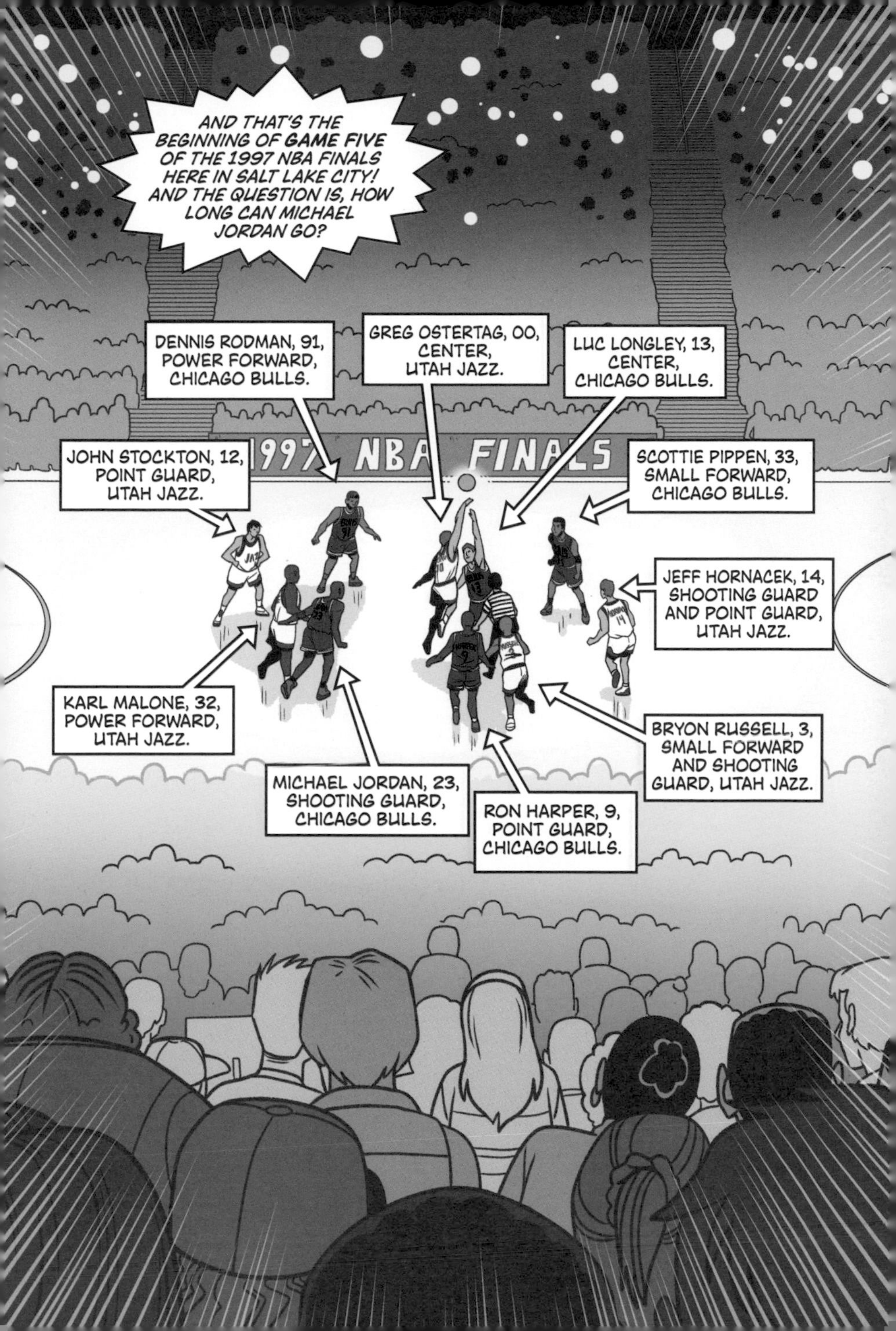
AND THAT'S THE BEGINNING OF **GAME FIVE** OF THE 1997 NBA FINALS HERE IN SALT LAKE CITY! AND THE QUESTION IS, HOW LONG CAN MICHAEL JORDAN GO?
DENNIS RODMAN, 91, POWER FORWARD, CHICAGO BULLS.
GREG OSTERTAG, 00, CENTER, UTAH JAZZ.
LUC LONGLEY, 13, CENTER, CHICAGO BULLS.
1997 NBA FINALS
JOHN STOCKTON, 12, POINT GUARD, UTAH JAZZ.
SCOTTIE PIPPEN, 33, SMALL FORWARD, CHICAGO BULLS.
JEFF HORNACEK, 14, SHOOTING GUARD AND POINT GUARD, UTAH JAZZ.
KARL MALONE, 32, POWER FORWARD, UTAH JAZZ.
BRYON RUSSELL, 3, SMALL FORWARD AND SHOOTING GUARD, UTAH JAZZ.
MICHAEL JORDAN, 23, SHOOTING GUARD, CHICAGO BULLS.
RON HARPER, 9, POINT GUARD, CHICAGO BULLS.

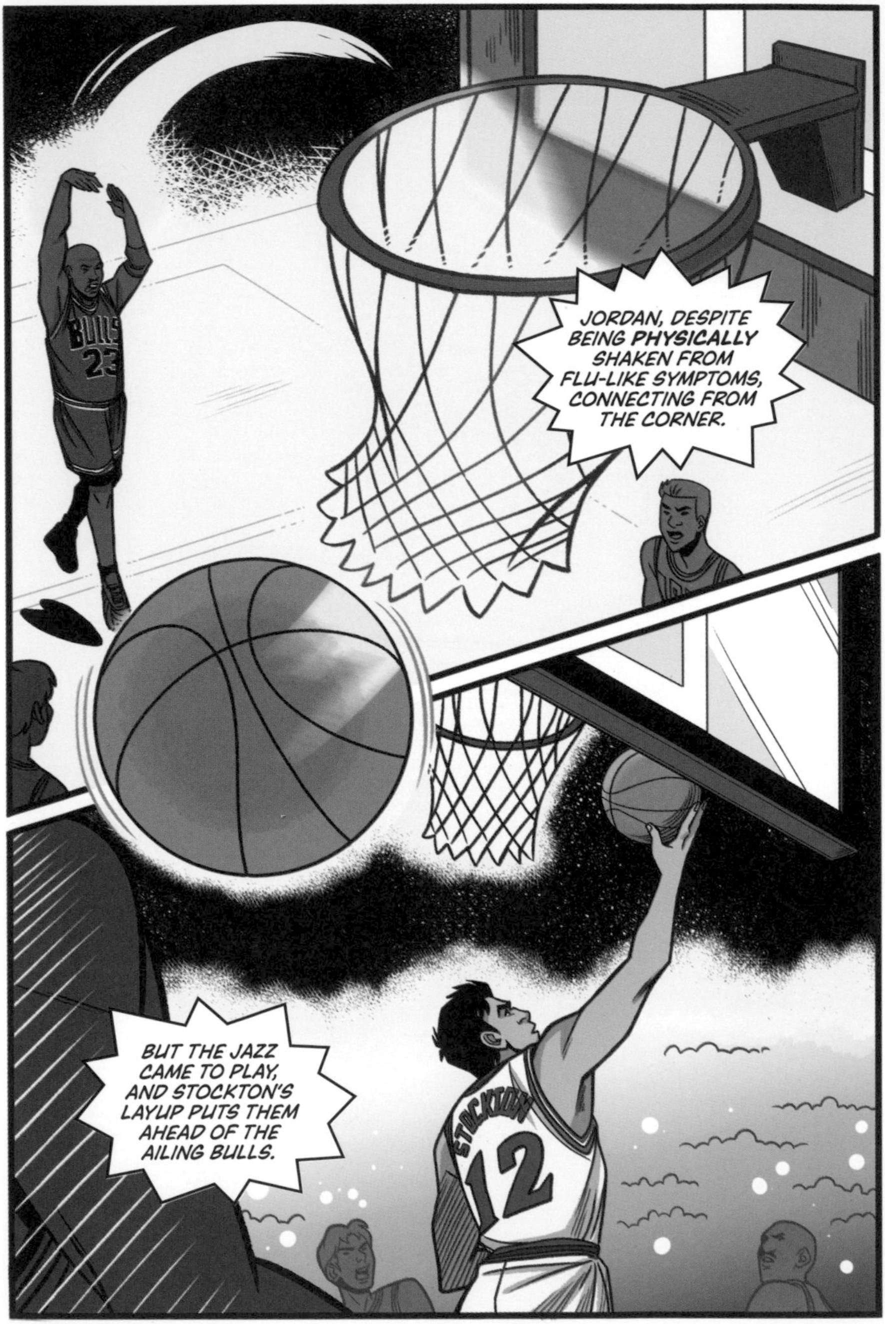
JORDAN, DESPITE BEING PHYSICALLY SHAKEN FROM FLU-LIKE SYMPTOMS, CONNECTING FROM THE CORNER.
BULLS 23
BUT THE JAZZ CAME TO PLAY, AND STOCKTON'S LAYUP PUTS THEM AHEAD OF THE AILING BULLS.
STOCKTON 12

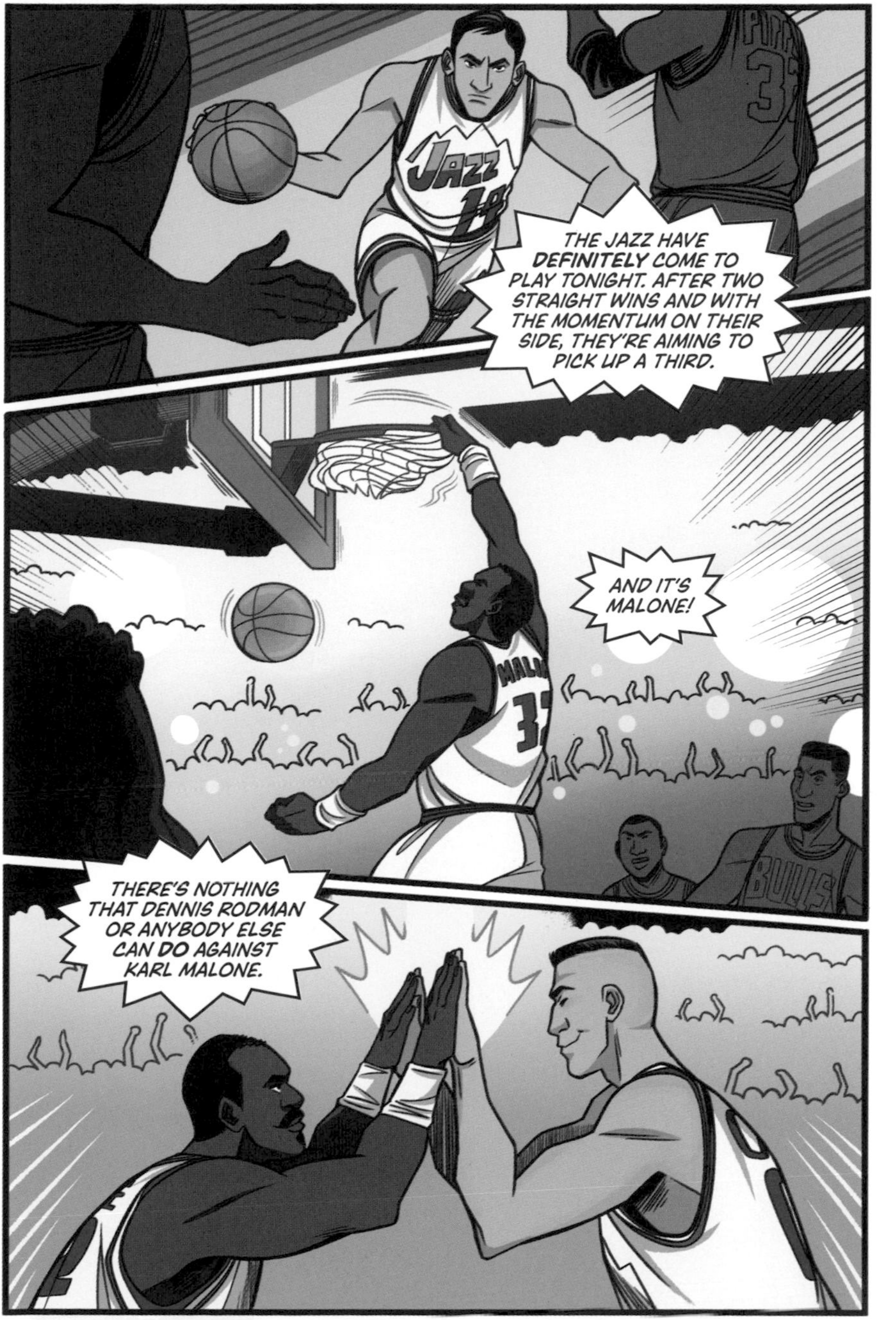
JAZZ
14
THE JAZZ HAVE DEFINITELY COME TO PLAY TONIGHT. AFTER TWO STRAIGHT WINS AND WITH THE MOMENTUM ON THEIR SIDE, THEY'RE AIMING TO PICK UP A THIRD.
AND IT'S MALONE!
BULLS
THERE'S NOTHING THAT DENNIS RODMAN OR ANYBODY ELSE CAN DO AGAINST KARL MALONE.

Karl Malone

The Chicago Bulls' path to victory in the 1997 NBA Finals was far from secure. Their opponents, the Utah Jazz (the team was originally based in New Orleans, hence the name) were the champions of the NBA Western Conference and were led by Karl Malone. The Louisiana-born power forward was known by the nickname "The Mailman," which he received while playing college basketball and referred to his ability to "deliver" points while under pressure. Malone began his NBA career with the Jazz in 1985. In the summer of 1992, Malone played alongside Michael Jordan, Scottie Pippen, and Jazz teammate John Stockton on the "Dream Team" in the 1992 Summer Olympics, winning a gold medal. In 1996, he returned to play on the Olympic team and once again earned top honors. Another player who is considered one of the greatest to ever play professional basketball, he eventually retired from the NBA in 2005 after almost twenty seasons on the courts.

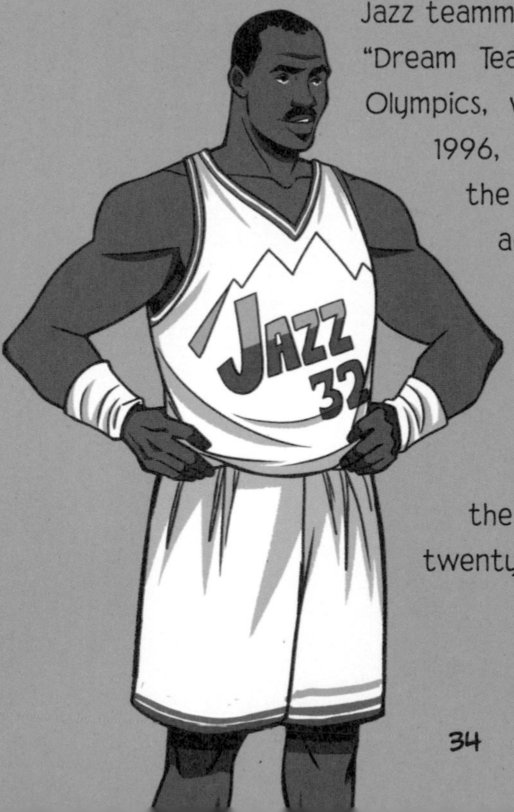
JAZZ
32

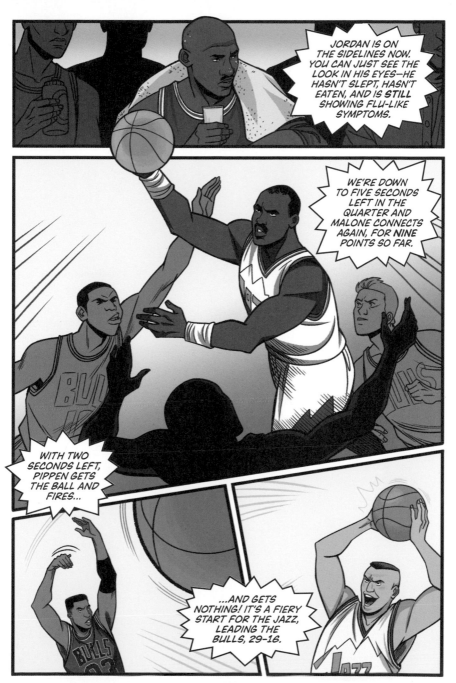

JORDAN IS ON THE SIDELINES NOW. YOU CAN JUST SEE THE LOOK IN HIS EYES—HE HASN'T SLEPT, HASN'T EATEN, AND IS **STILL** SHOWING FLU-LIKE SYMPTOMS.

WE'RE DOWN TO FIVE SECONDS LEFT IN THE QUARTER AND MALONE CONNECTS AGAIN, FOR **NINE** POINTS SO FAR.

WITH TWO SECONDS LEFT, PIPPEN GETS THE BALL AND FIRES...

...AND GETS NOTHING! IT'S A FIERY START FOR THE JAZZ, LEADING THE BULLS, 29-16.

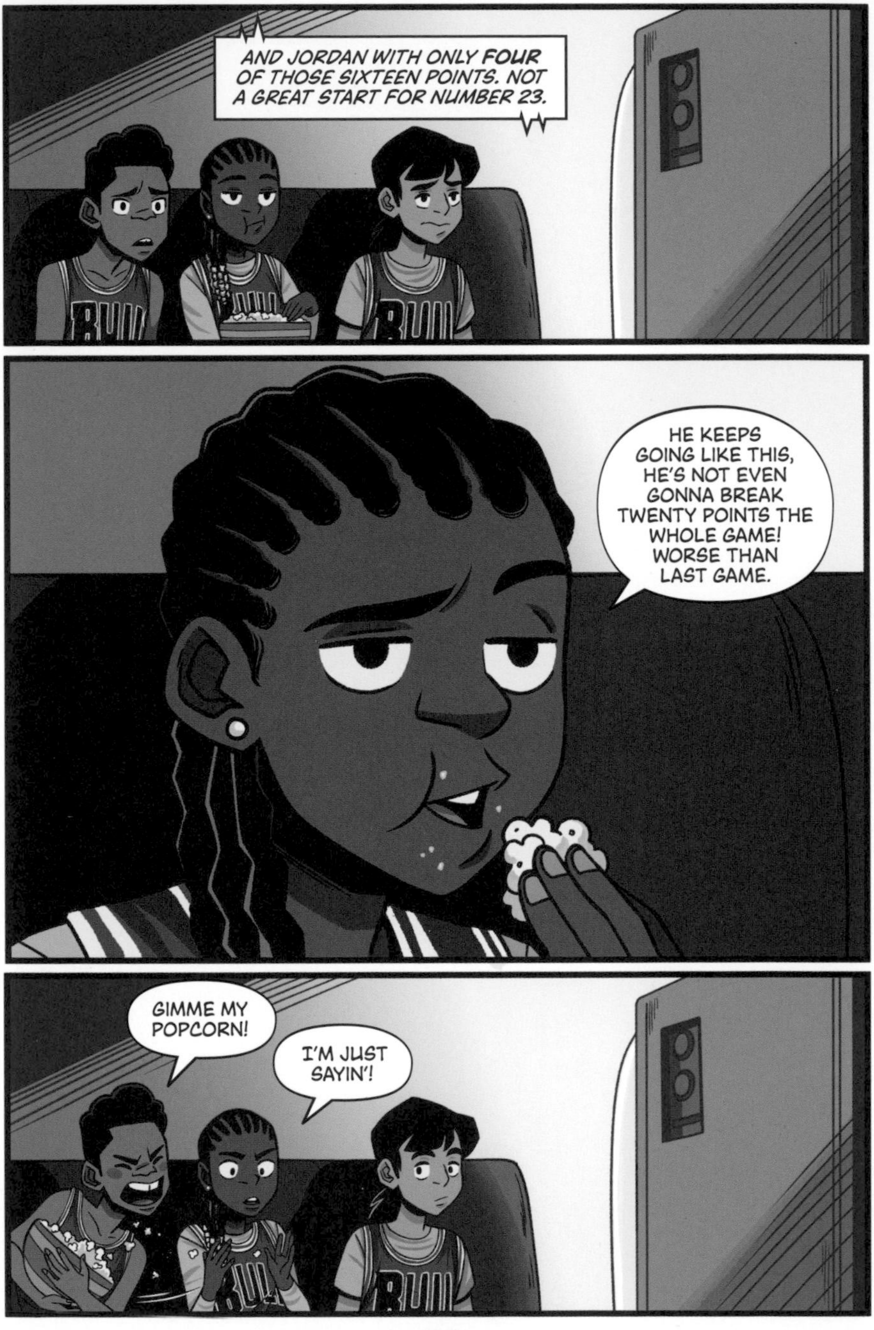
AND JORDAN WITH ONLY **FOUR** OF THOSE SIXTEEN POINTS. NOT A GREAT START FOR NUMBER 23.
HE KEEPS GOING LIKE THIS, HE'S NOT EVEN GONNA BREAK TWENTY POINTS THE WHOLE GAME! WORSE THAN LAST GAME.
GIMME MY POPCORN!
I'M JUST SAYIN'!

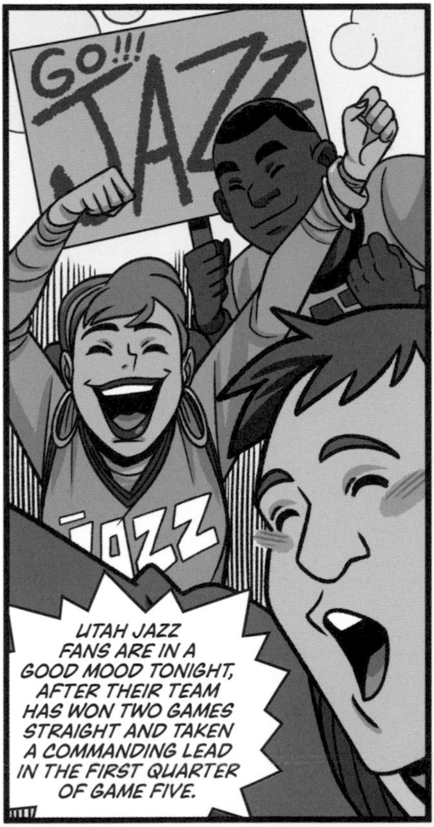
GO!!! JAZZ
JAZZ
UTAH JAZZ FANS ARE IN A GOOD MOOD TONIGHT, AFTER THEIR TEAM HAS WON TWO GAMES STRAIGHT AND TAKEN A COMMANDING LEAD IN THE FIRST QUARTER OF GAME FIVE.

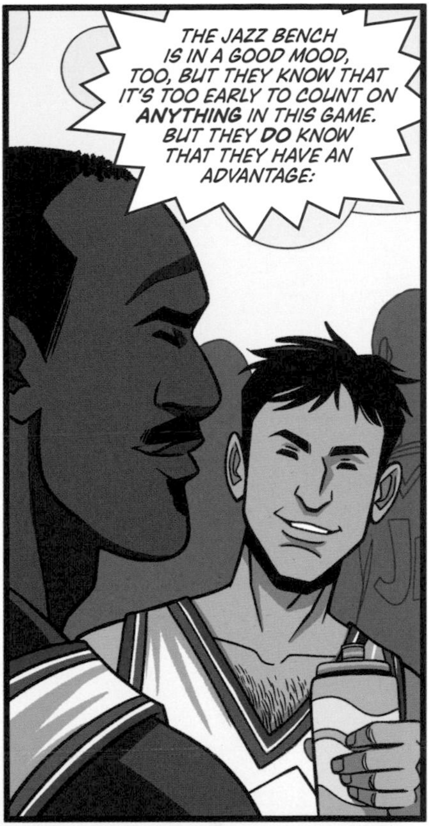
THE JAZZ BENCH IS IN A GOOD MOOD, TOO, BUT THEY KNOW THAT IT'S TOO EARLY TO COUNT ON **ANYTHING** IN THIS GAME. BUT THEY **DO** KNOW THAT THEY HAVE AN ADVANTAGE:

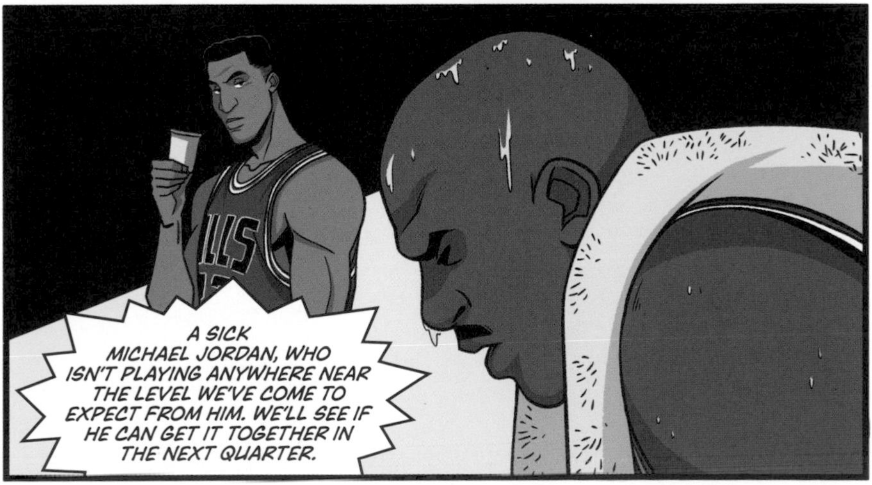
A SICK MICHAEL JORDAN, WHO ISN'T PLAYING ANYWHERE NEAR THE LEVEL WE'VE COME TO EXPECT FROM HIM. WE'LL SEE IF HE CAN GET IT TOGETHER IN THE NEXT QUARTER.

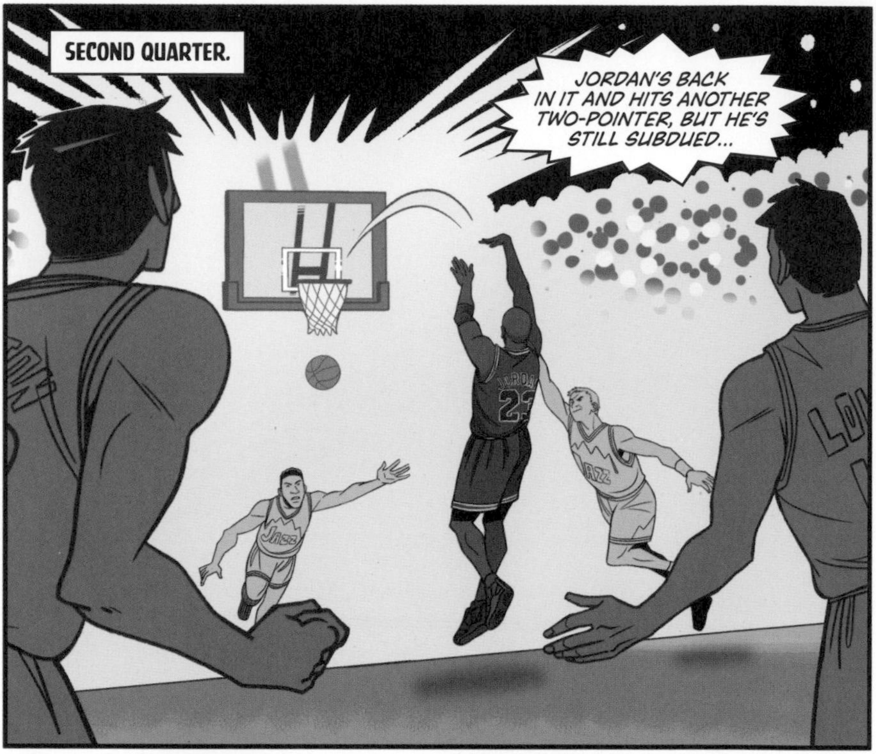
SECOND QUARTER.
JORDAN'S BACK IN IT AND HITS ANOTHER TWO-POINTER, BUT HE'S STILL SUBDUED...
JORDAN
23
JAZZ

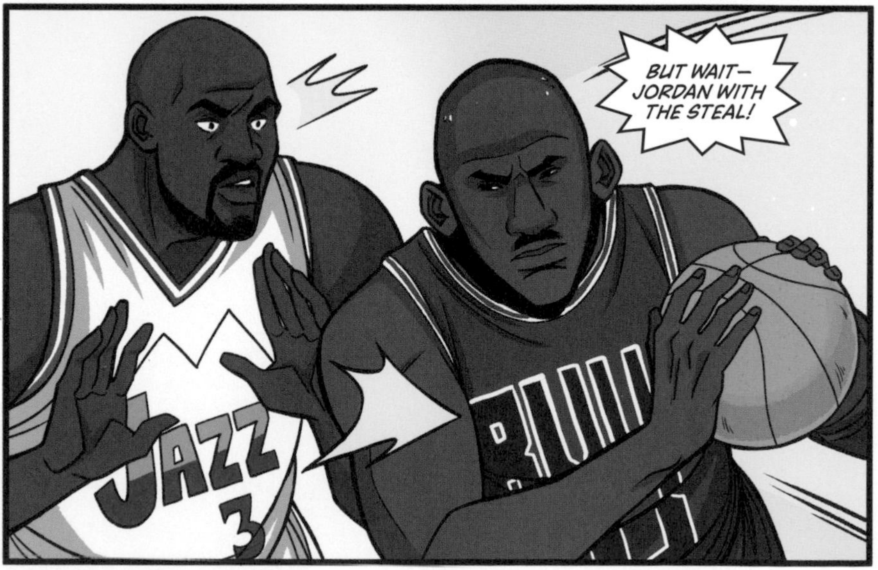
BUT WAIT—JORDAN WITH THE STEAL!
JAZZ
3

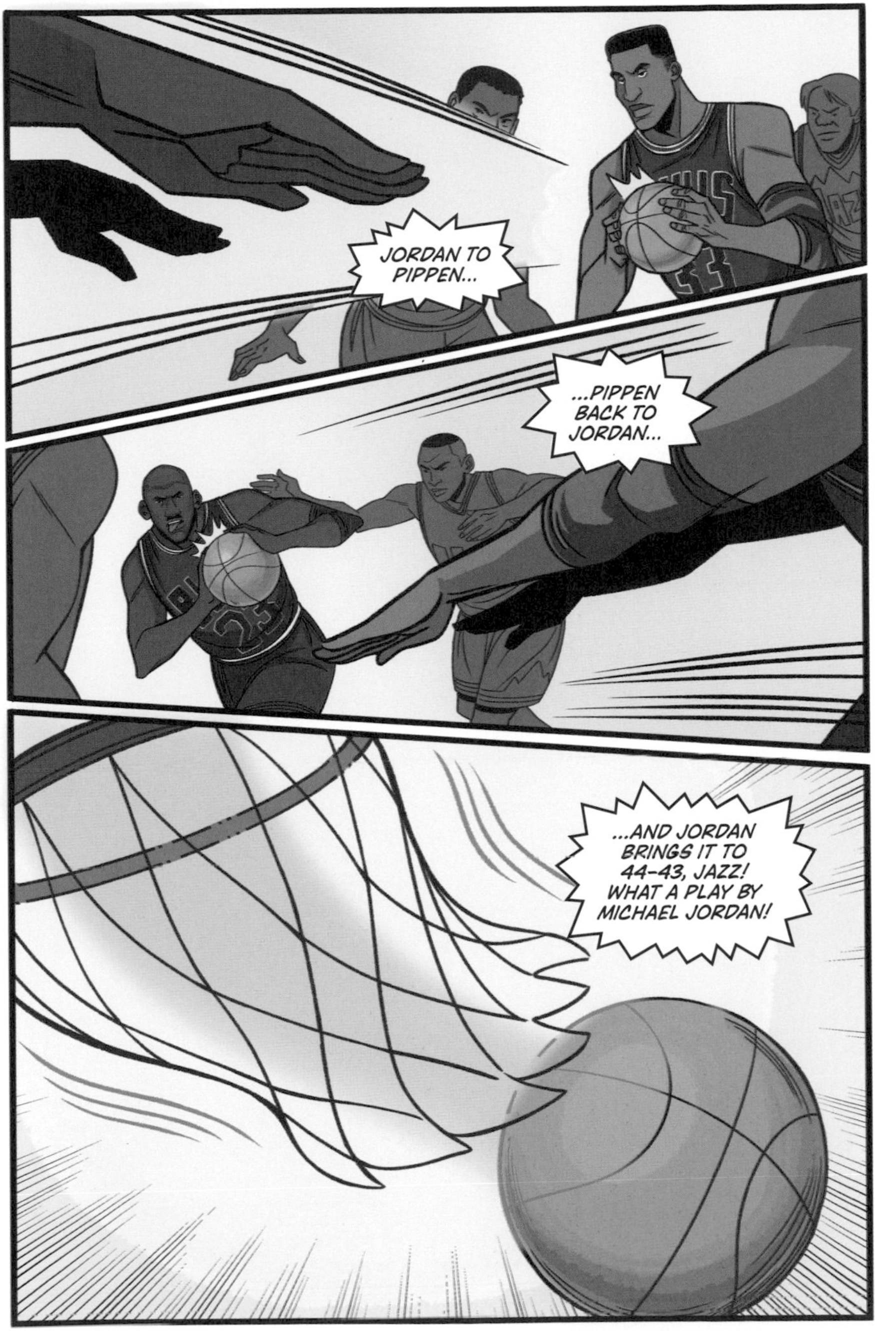
JORDAN TO PIPPEN...
...PIPPEN BACK TO JORDAN...
...AND JORDAN BRINGS IT TO 44-43, JAZZ! WHAT A PLAY BY MICHAEL JORDAN!

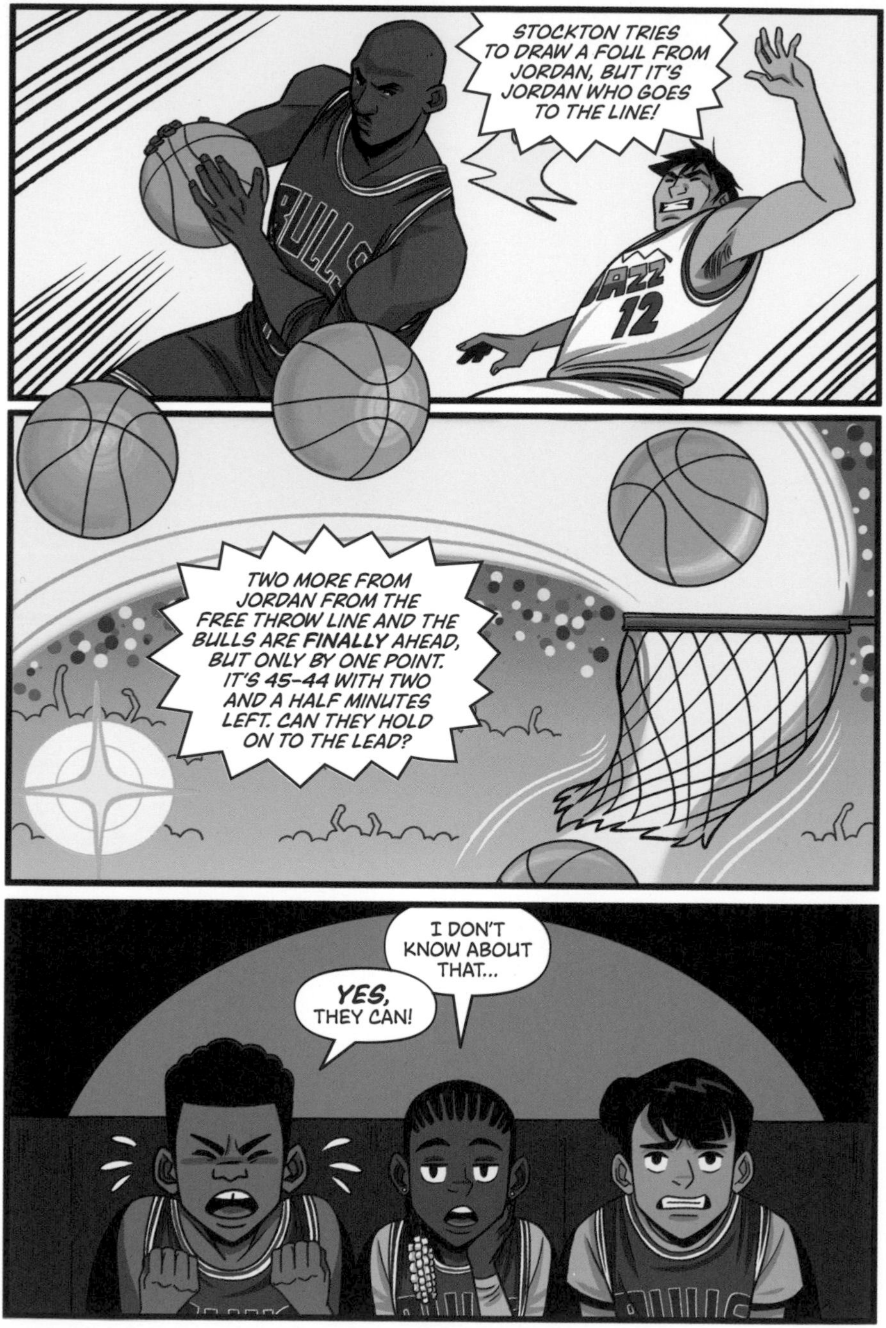
STOCKTON TRIES TO DRAW A FOUL FROM JORDAN, BUT IT'S JORDAN WHO GOES TO THE LINE!
BULLS
JAZZ 12
TWO MORE FROM JORDAN FROM THE FREE THROW LINE AND THE BULLS ARE FINALLY AHEAD, BUT ONLY BY ONE POINT. IT'S 45–44 WITH TWO AND A HALF MINUTES LEFT. CAN THEY HOLD ON TO THE LEAD?
YES, THEY CAN!
I DON'T KNOW ABOUT THAT...

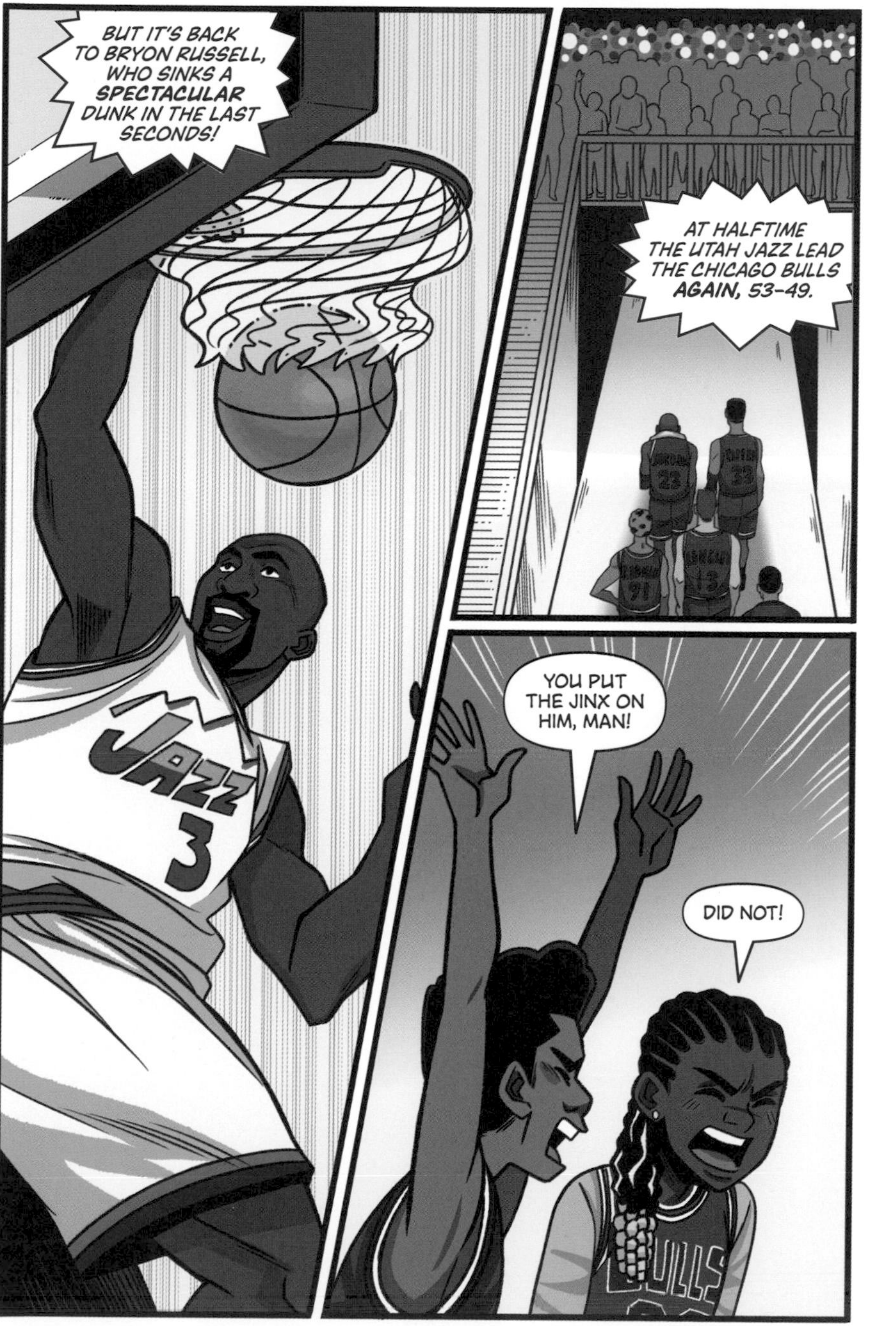
BUT IT'S BACK TO BRYON RUSSELL, WHO SINKS A SPECTACULAR DUNK IN THE LAST SECONDS!
JAZZ
3
AT HALFTIME THE UTAH JAZZ LEAD THE CHICAGO BULLS AGAIN, 53–49.
YOU PUT THE JINX ON HIM, MAN!
DID NOT!

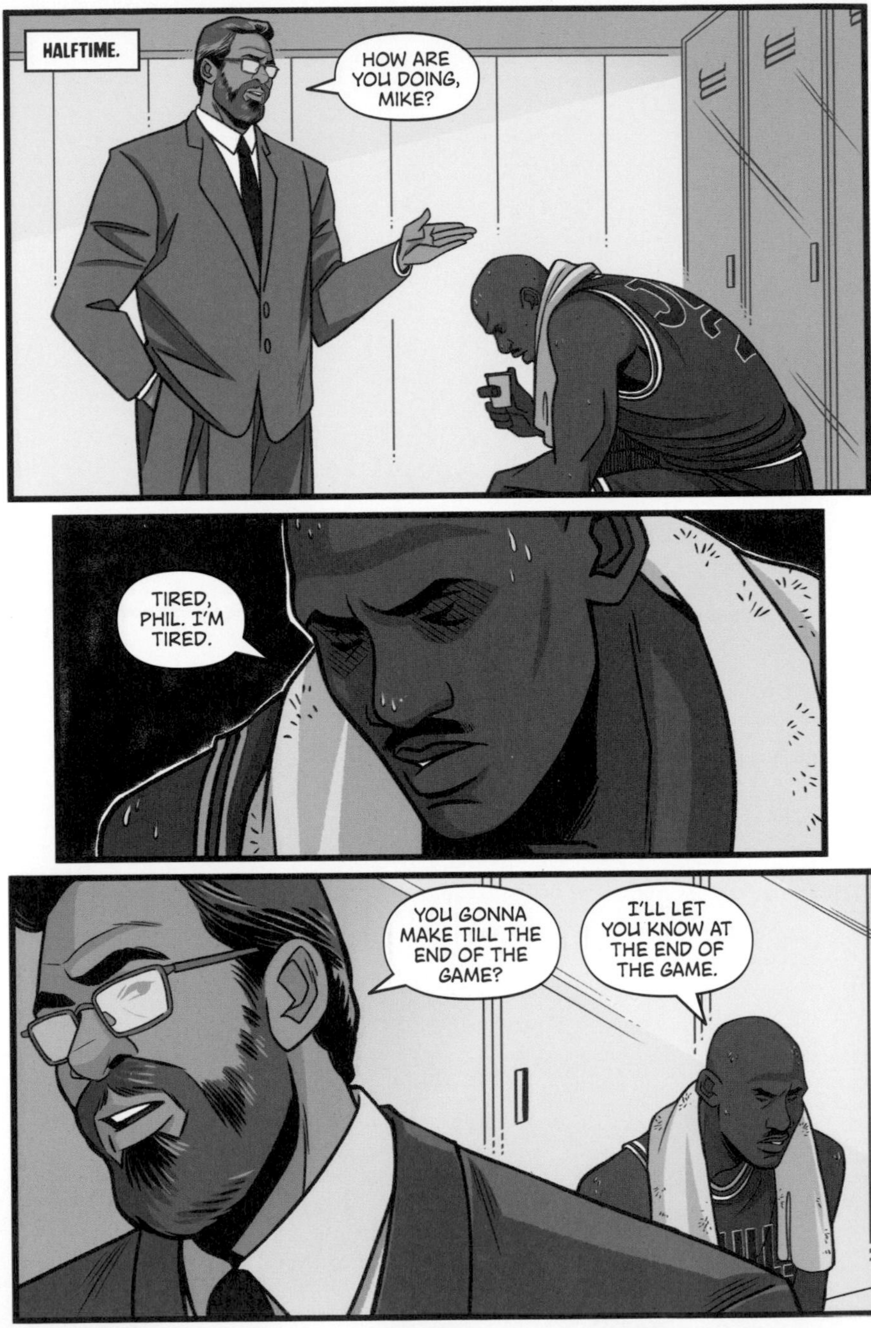
HALFTIME.
HOW ARE YOU DOING, MIKE?
TIRED, PHIL. I'M TIRED.
YOU GONNA MAKE TILL THE END OF THE GAME?
I'LL LET YOU KNOW AT THE END OF THE GAME.

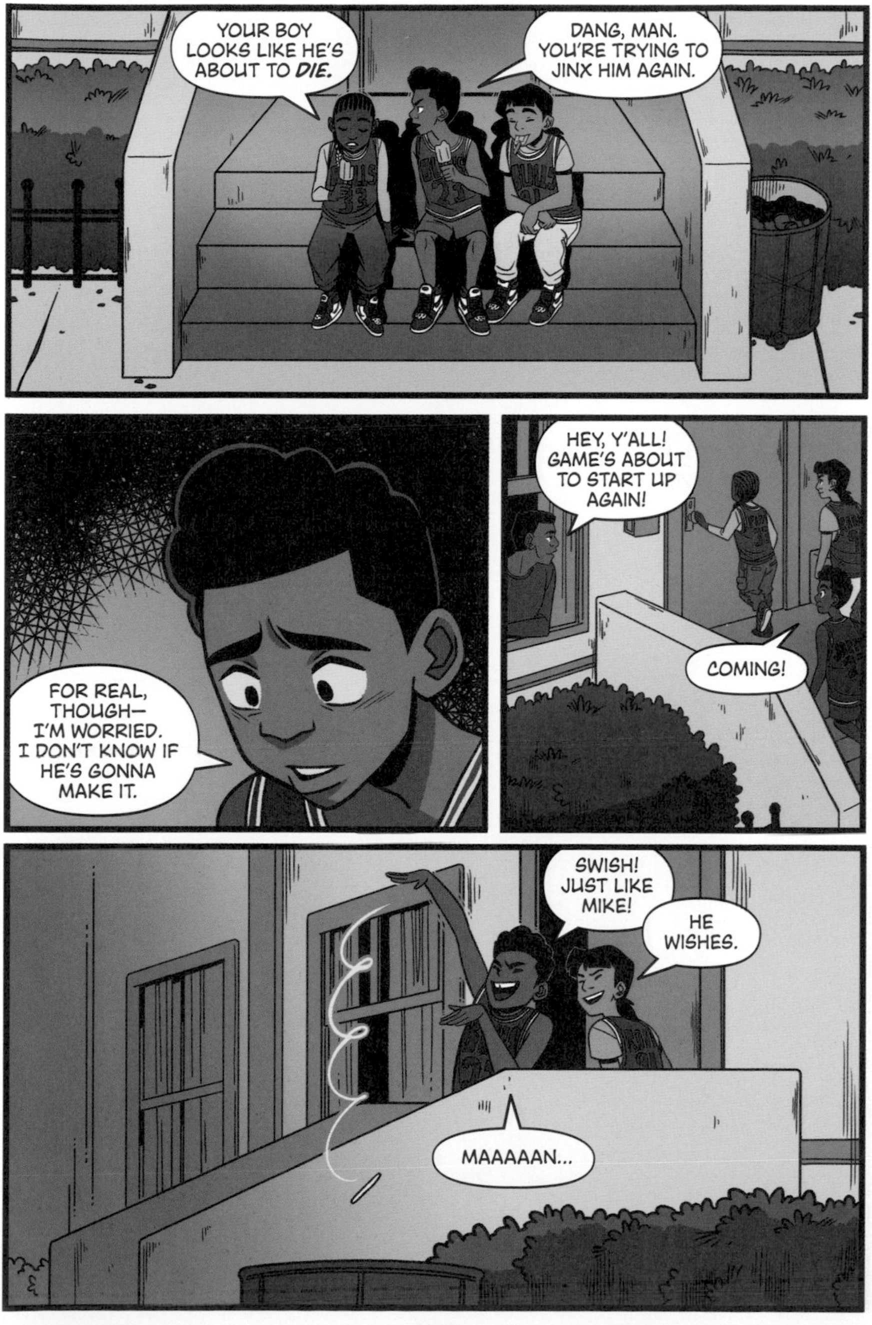
YOUR BOY LOOKS LIKE HE'S ABOUT TO *DIE.*
DANG, MAN. YOU'RE TRYING TO JINX HIM AGAIN.
FOR REAL, THOUGH— I'M WORRIED. I DON'T KNOW IF HE'S GONNA MAKE IT.
HEY, Y'ALL! GAME'S ABOUT TO START UP AGAIN!
COMING!
SWISH! JUST LIKE MIKE!
HE WISHES.
MAAAAAN...

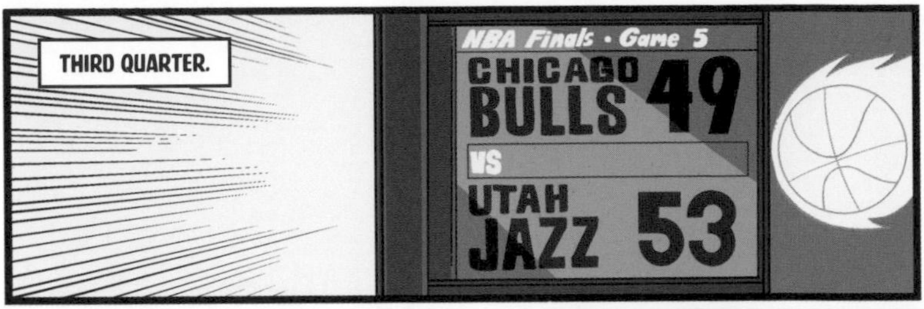
THIRD QUARTER.
NBA Finals • Game 5
CHICAGO BULLS 49
VS
UTAH JAZZ 53

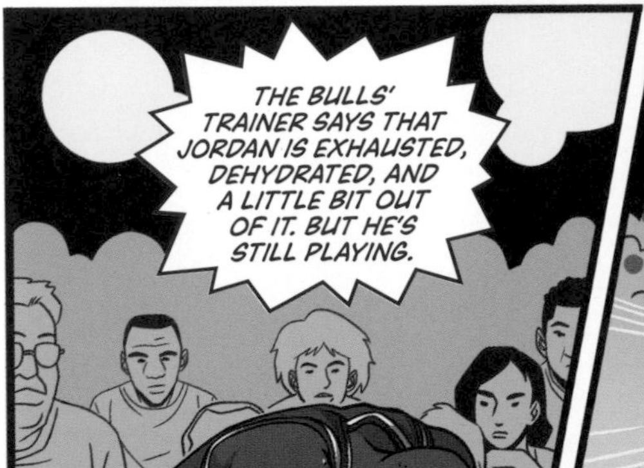
THE BULLS' TRAINER SAYS THAT JORDAN IS EXHAUSTED, DEHYDRATED, AND A LITTLE BIT OUT OF IT. BUT HE'S STILL PLAYING.

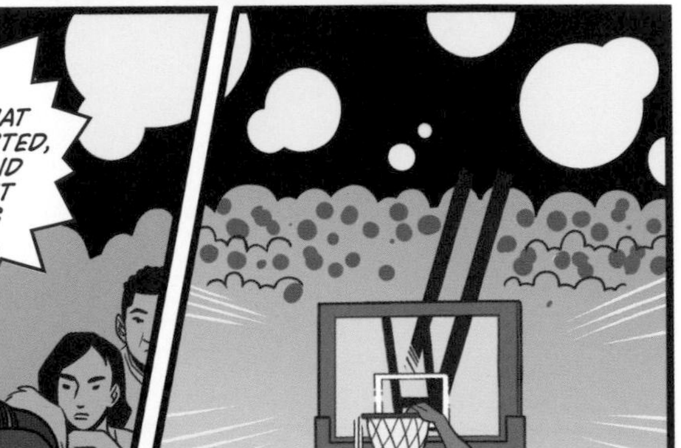

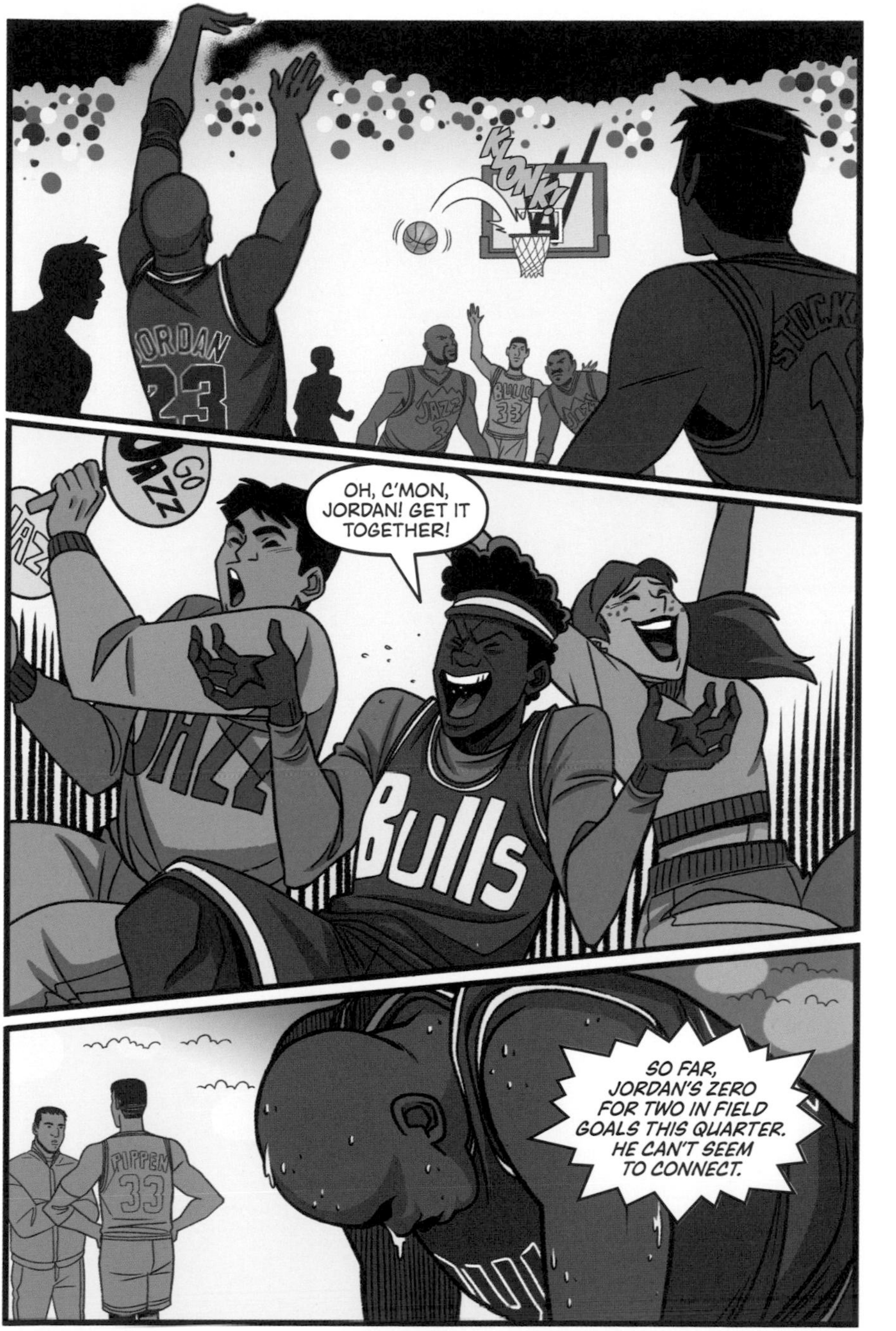
KLONK!
OH, C'MON, JORDAN! GET IT TOGETHER!
SO FAR, JORDAN'S ZERO FOR TWO IN FIELD GOALS THIS QUARTER. HE CAN'T SEEM TO CONNECT.

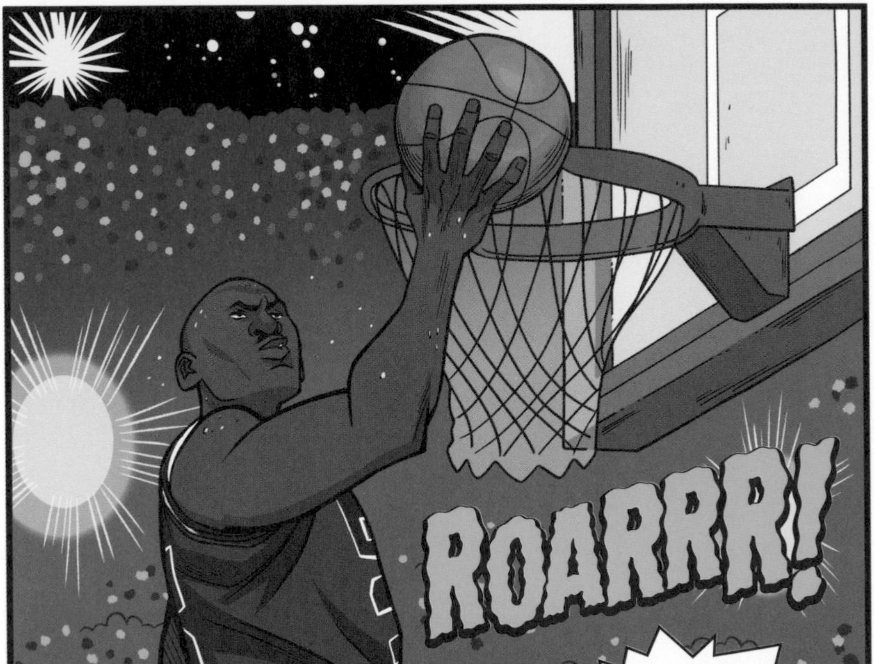
ROARRR!
BUT THERE'S A LITTLE FLASH OF THE JORDAN WE KNOW!

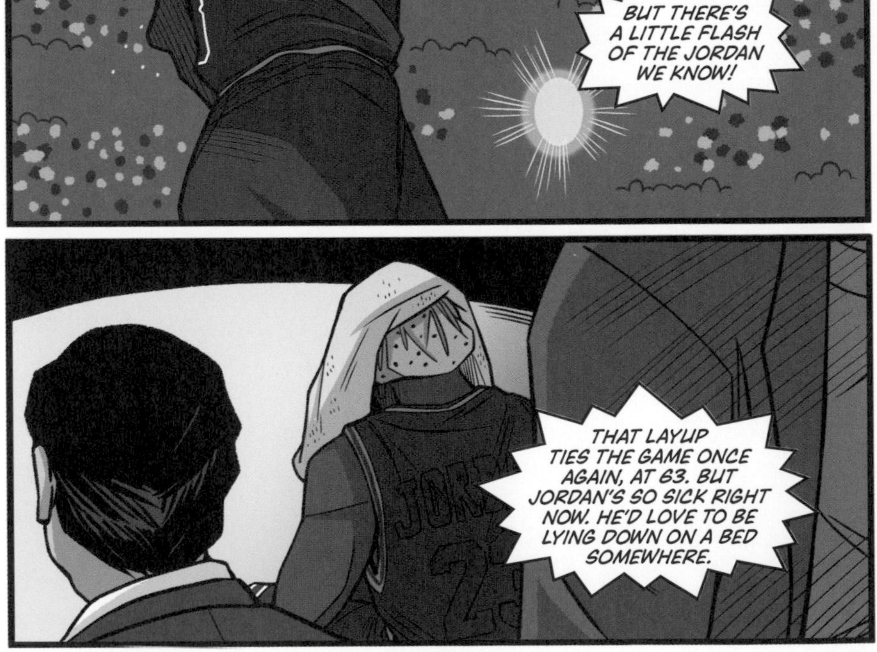
THAT LAYUP TIES THE GAME ONCE AGAIN, AT 63. BUT JORDAN'S SO SICK RIGHT NOW. HE'D LOVE TO BE LYING DOWN ON A BED SOMEWHERE.

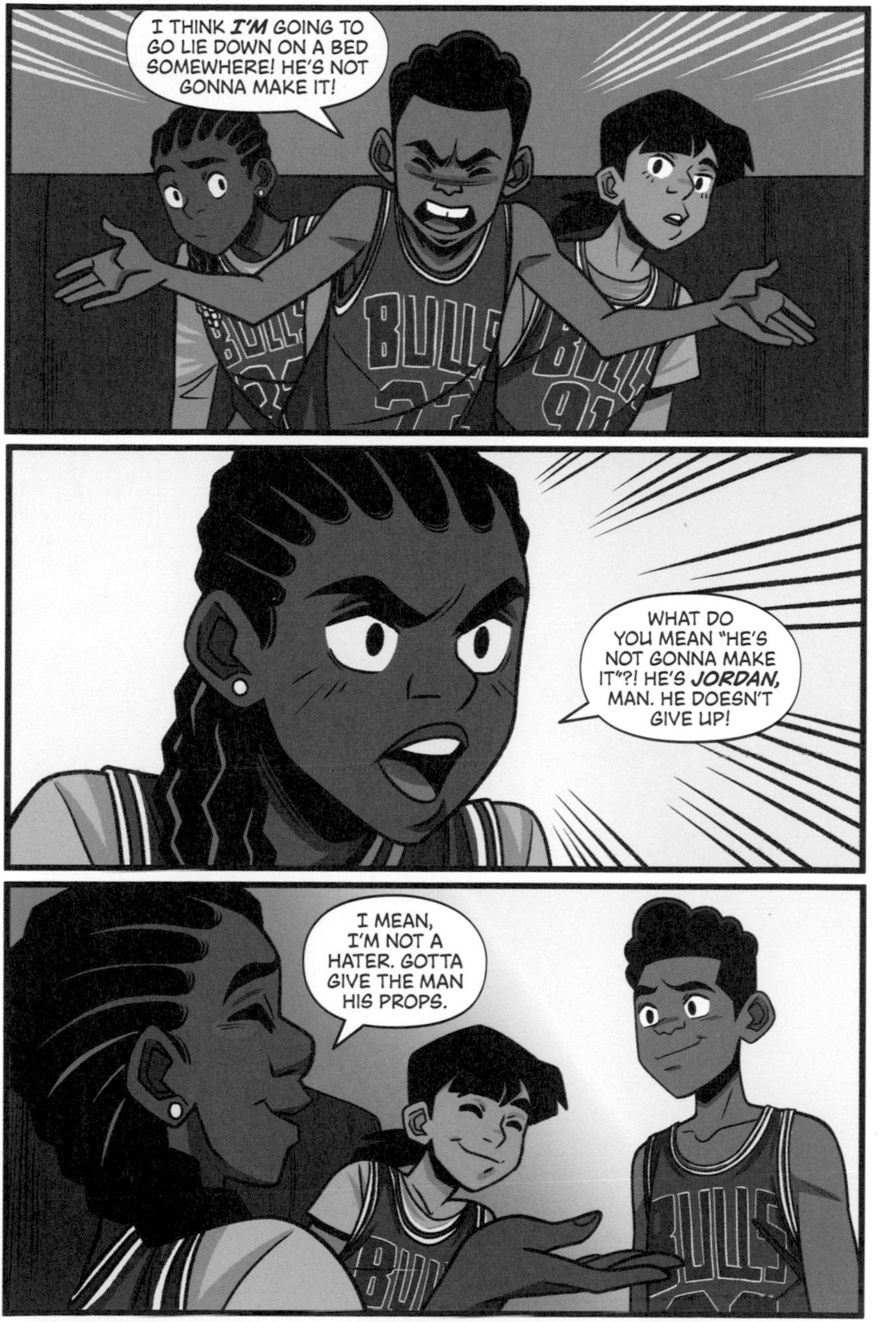
I THINK *I'M* GOING TO GO LIE DOWN ON A BED SOMEWHERE! HE'S NOT GONNA MAKE IT!
BULLS
BULLS
BULLS
WHAT DO YOU MEAN "HE'S NOT GONNA MAKE IT"?! HE'S *JORDAN,* MAN. HE DOESN'T GIVE UP!
I MEAN, I'M NOT A HATER. GOTTA GIVE THE MAN HIS PROPS.
BULLS
BULLS

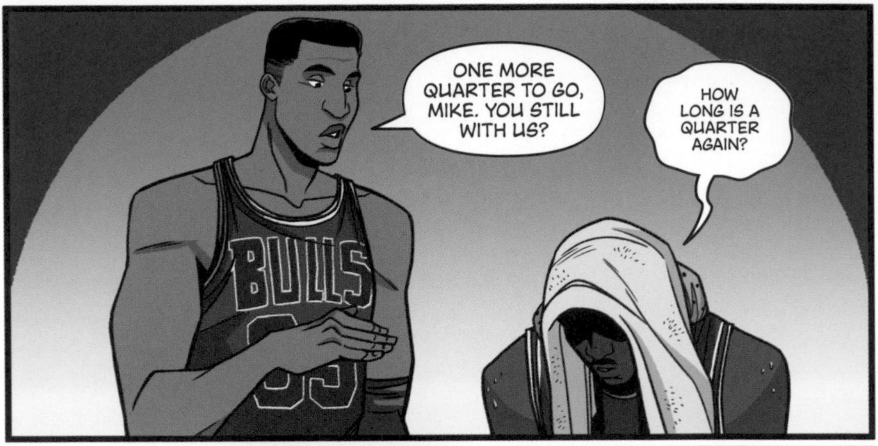
ONE MORE QUARTER TO GO, MIKE. YOU STILL WITH US?
HOW LONG IS A QUARTER AGAIN?

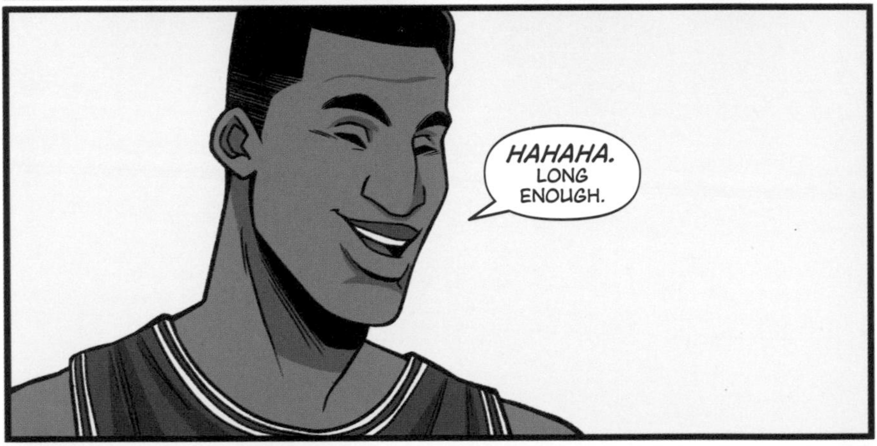
HAHAHA. LONG ENOUGH.

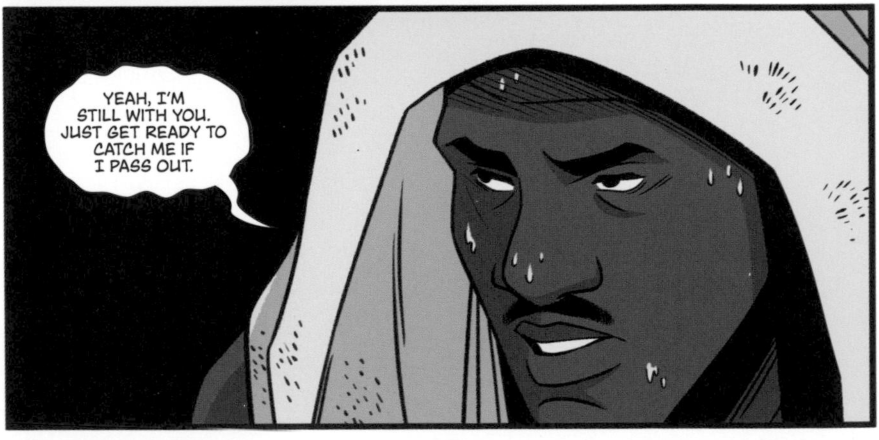
YEAH, I'M STILL WITH YOU. JUST GET READY TO CATCH ME IF I PASS OUT.

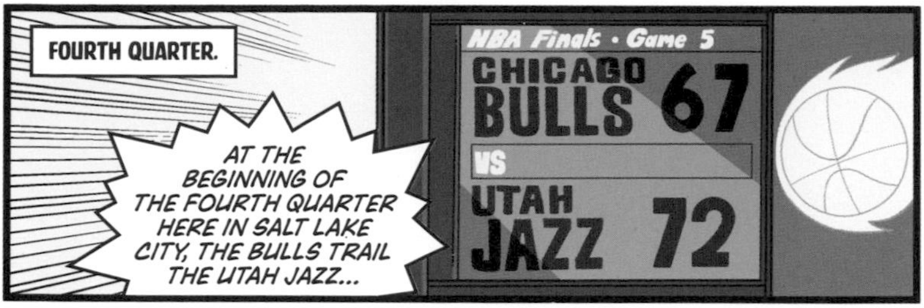
FOURTH QUARTER.
AT THE BEGINNING OF THE FOURTH QUARTER HERE IN SALT LAKE CITY, THE BULLS TRAIL THE UTAH JAZZ...
NBA Finals • Game 5
CHICAGO BULLS 67
VS
UTAH JAZZ 72

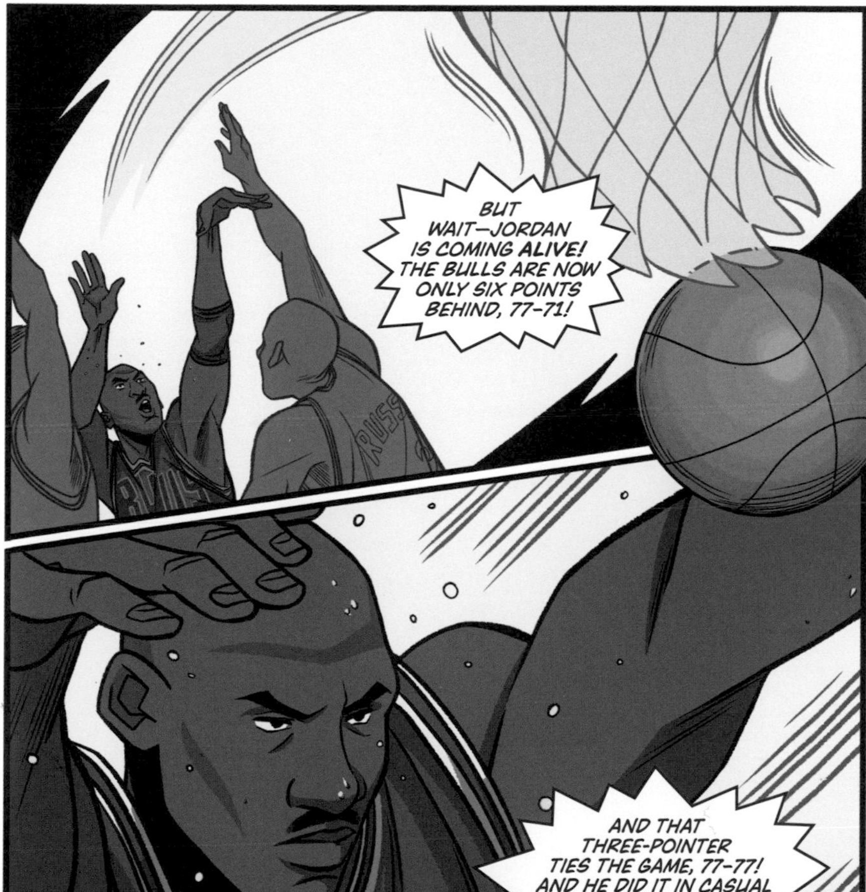
BUT WAIT—JORDAN IS COMING ALIVE! THE BULLS ARE NOW ONLY SIX POINTS BEHIND, 77–71!
AND THAT THREE-POINTER TIES THE GAME, 77–77! AND HE DID IT IN CASUAL FORM—AND YOU COULD SEE HOW EXHAUSTED MICHAEL JORDAN IS.

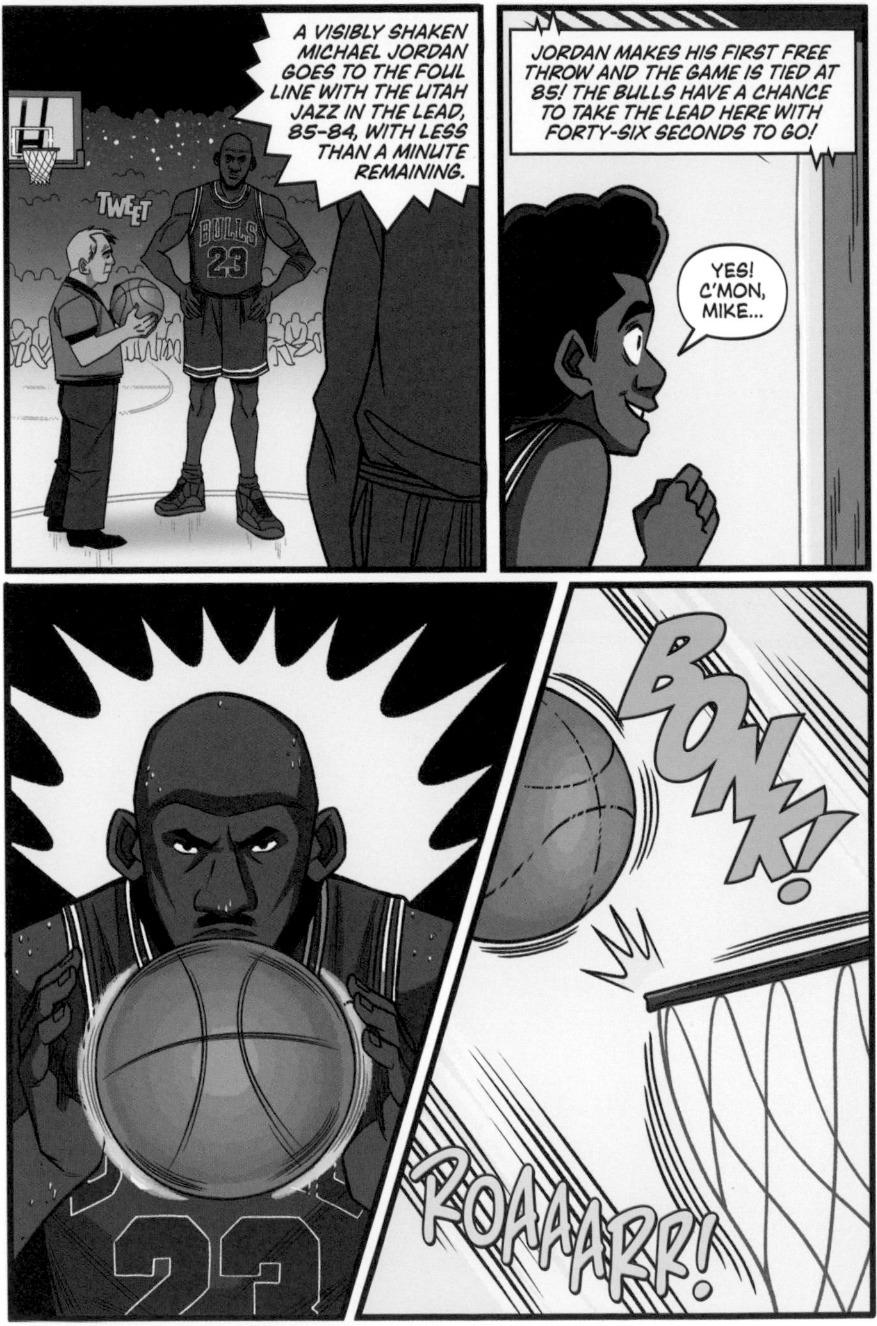

A VISIBLY SHAKEN MICHAEL JORDAN GOES TO THE FOUL LINE WITH THE UTAH JAZZ IN THE LEAD, 85-84, WITH LESS THAN A MINUTE REMAINING.
TWEET
BULLS 23
JORDAN MAKES HIS FIRST FREE THROW AND THE GAME IS TIED AT 85! THE BULLS HAVE A CHANCE TO TAKE THE LEAD HERE WITH FORTY-SIX SECONDS TO GO!
YES! C'MON, MIKE...
BONK!
ROAAAARR!

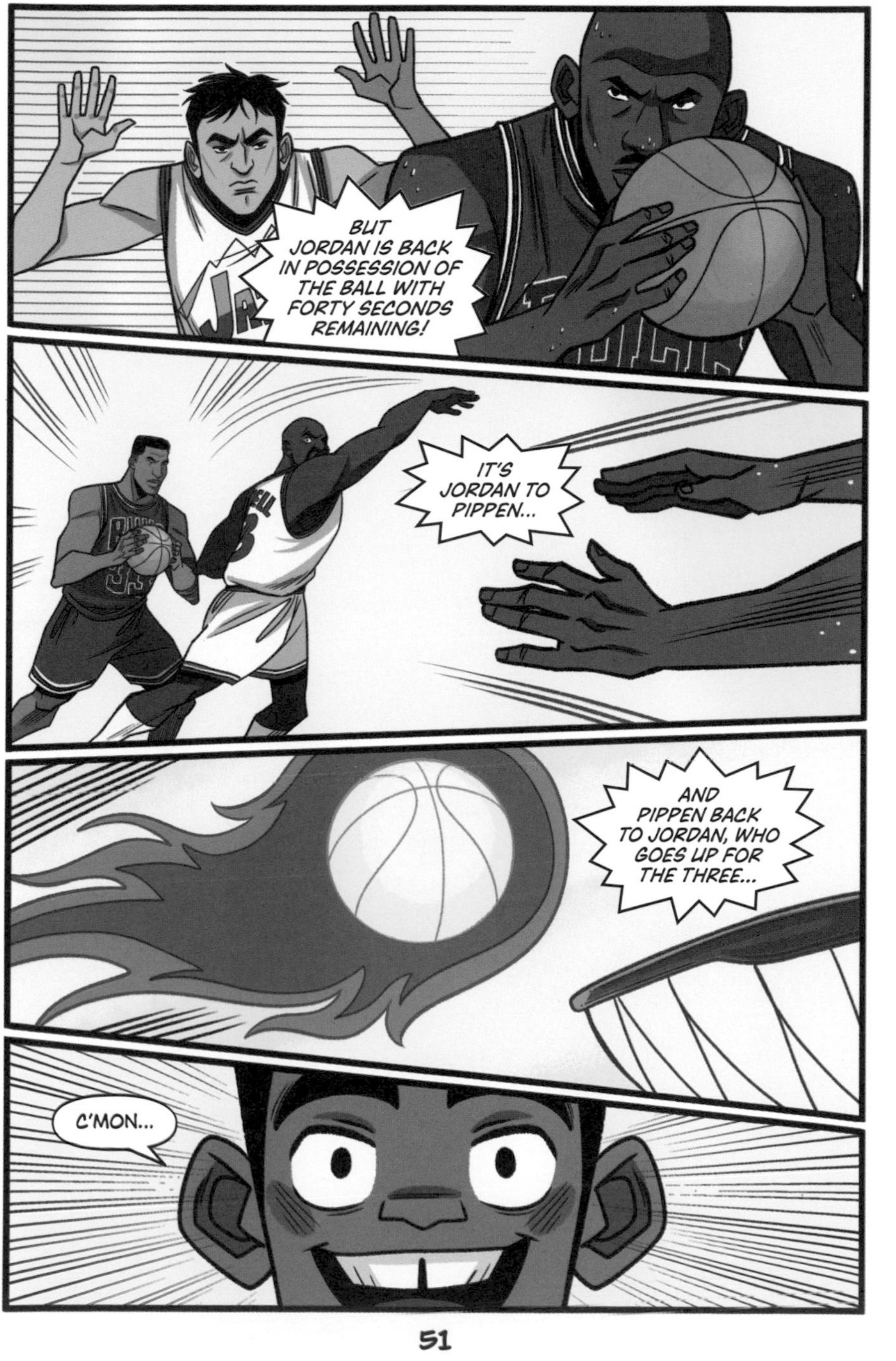
BUT JORDAN IS BACK IN POSSESSION OF THE BALL WITH FORTY SECONDS REMAINING!
IT'S JORDAN TO PIPPEN...
AND PIPPEN BACK TO JORDAN, WHO GOES UP FOR THE THREE...
C'MON...

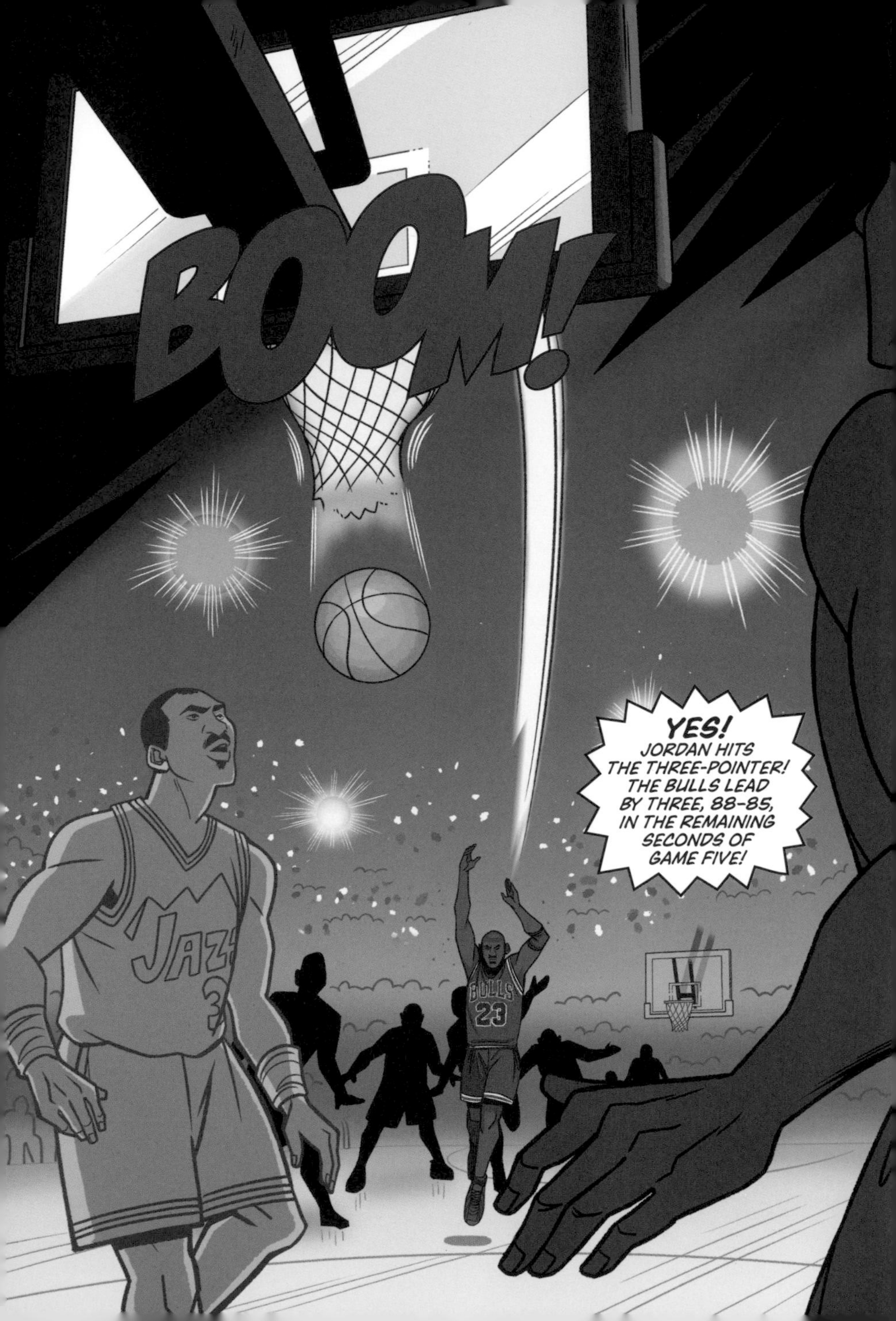
BOOM!
YES! JORDAN HITS THE THREE-POINTER! THE BULLS LEAD BY THREE, 88-85, IN THE REMAINING SECONDS OF GAME FIVE!
JAZZ 3
BULLS 23

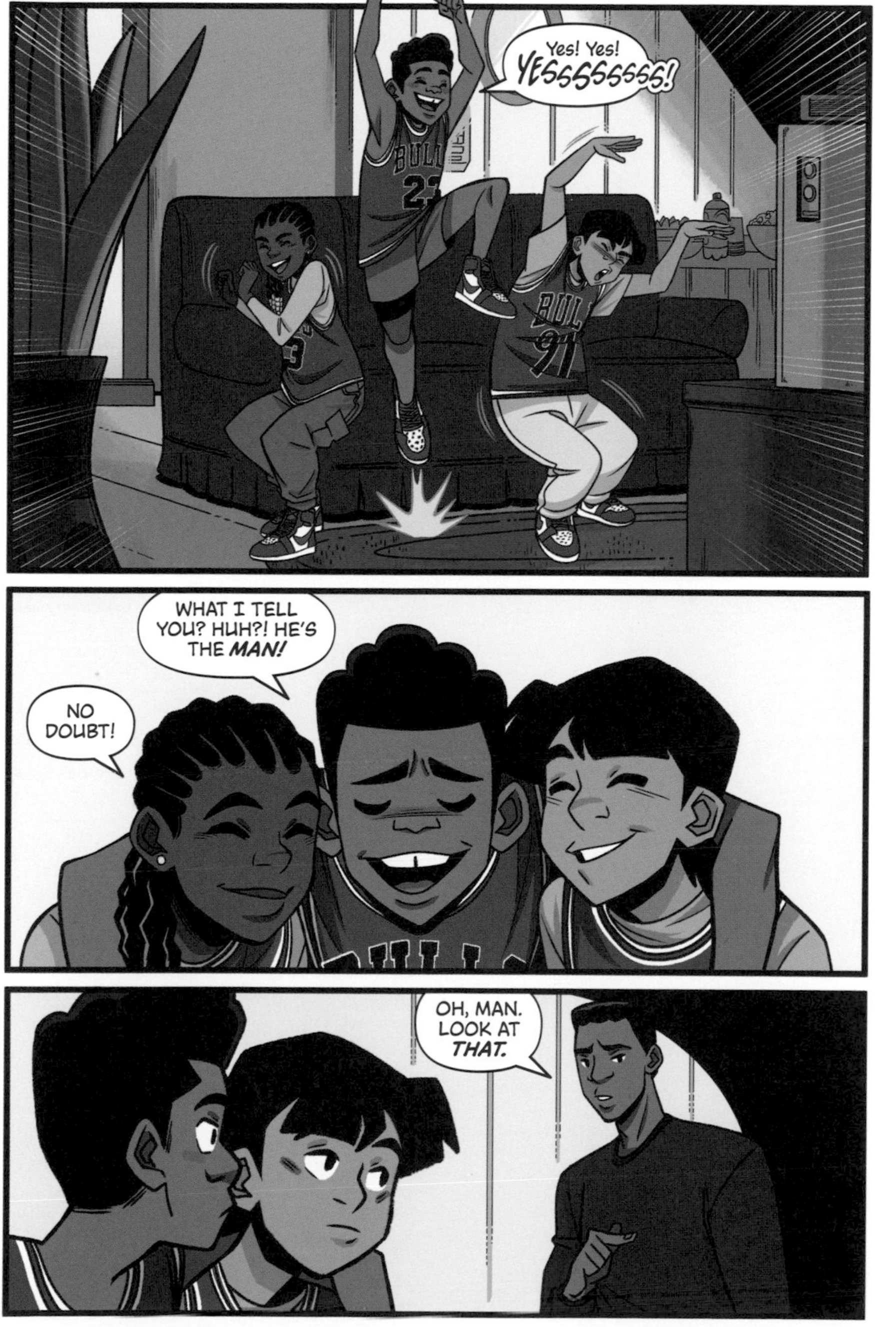

Yes! Yes! YESSSSSSSS!
WHAT I TELL YOU? HUH?! HE'S THE *MAN!*
NO DOUBT!
OH, MAN. LOOK AT *THAT.*

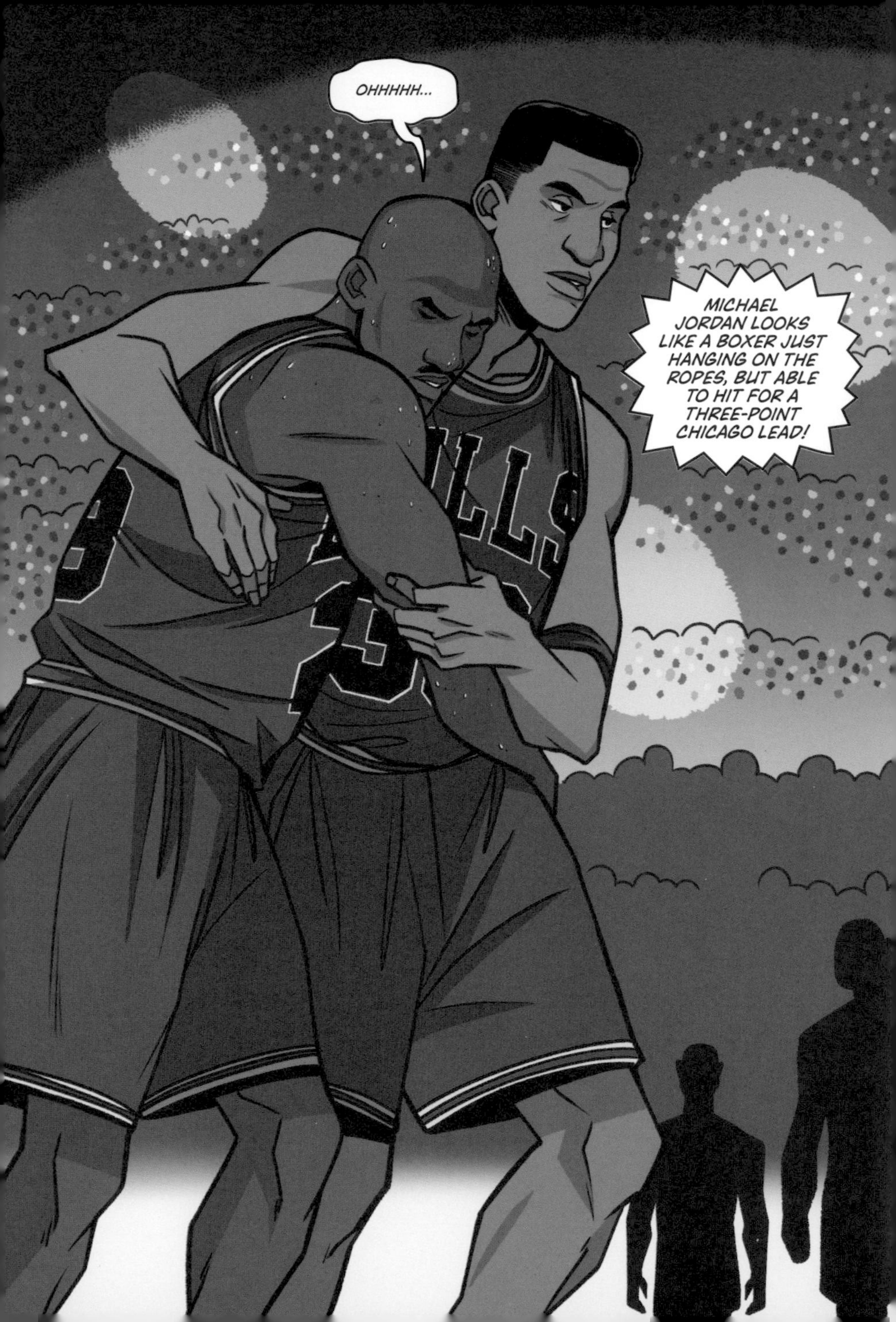
OHHHHH...
MICHAEL JORDAN LOOKS LIKE A BOXER JUST HANGING ON THE ROPES, BUT ABLE TO HIT FOR A THREE-POINT CHICAGO LEAD!
BULLS

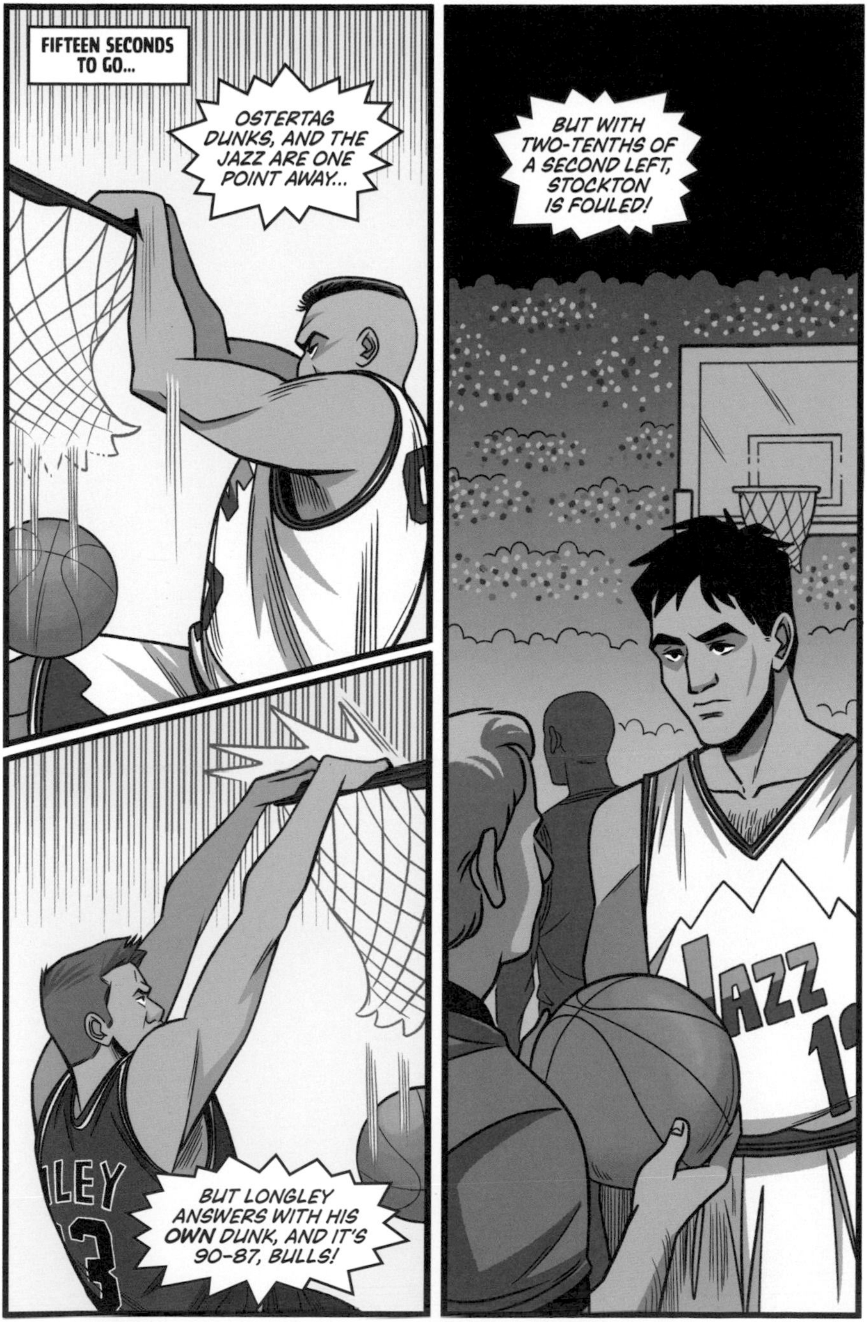
FIFTEEN SECONDS TO GO...
OSTERTAG DUNKS, AND THE JAZZ ARE ONE POINT AWAY...
BUT LONGLEY ANSWERS WITH HIS OWN DUNK, AND IT'S 90-87, BULLS!
LEY
BUT WITH TWO-TENTHS OF A SECOND LEFT, STOCKTON IS FOULED!
JAZZ

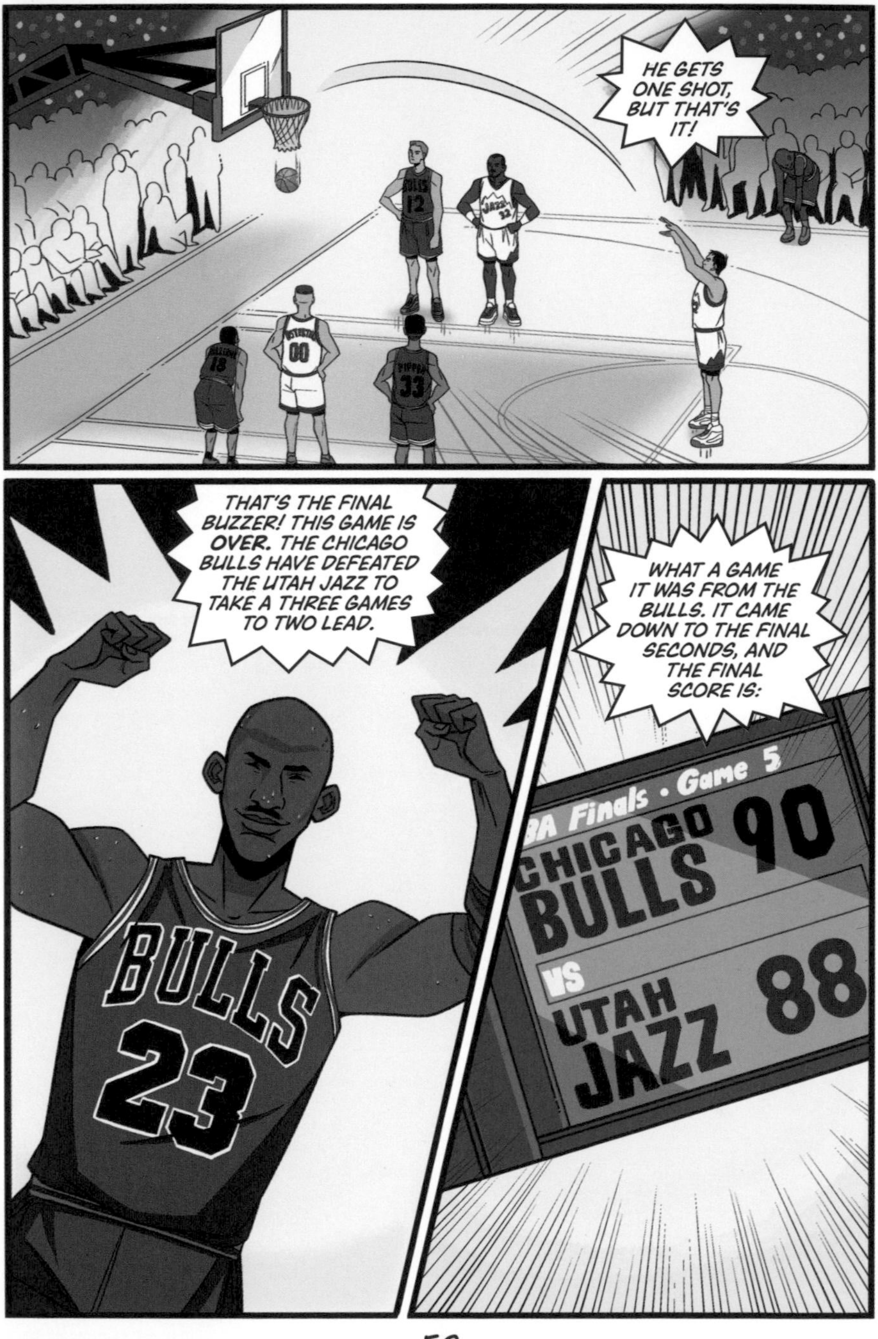
HE GETS ONE SHOT, BUT THAT'S IT!
THAT'S THE FINAL BUZZER! THIS GAME IS **OVER**. THE CHICAGO BULLS HAVE DEFEATED THE UTAH JAZZ TO TAKE A THREE GAMES TO TWO LEAD.
WHAT A GAME IT WAS FROM THE BULLS. IT CAME DOWN TO THE FINAL SECONDS, AND THE FINAL SCORE IS:
BA Finals • Game 5
CHICAGO BULLS 90
VS
UTAH JAZZ 88

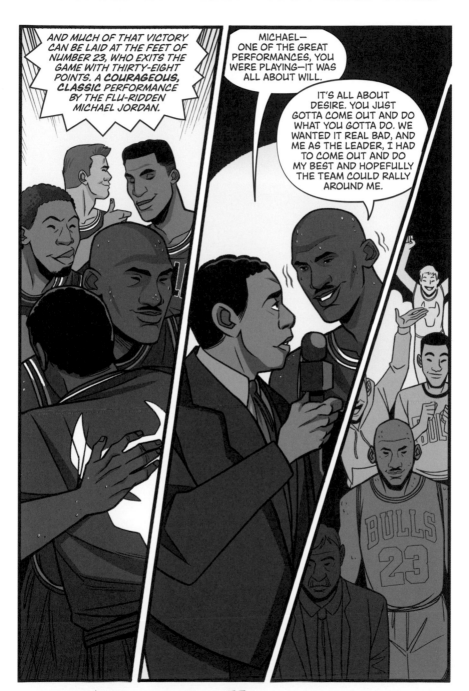

AND MUCH OF THAT VICTORY CAN BE LAID AT THE FEET OF NUMBER 23, WHO EXITS THE GAME WITH THIRTY-EIGHT POINTS. A *COURAGEOUS*, *CLASSIC* PERFORMANCE BY THE FLU-RIDDEN MICHAEL JORDAN.

MICHAEL— ONE OF THE GREAT PERFORMANCES, YOU WERE PLAYING—IT WAS ALL ABOUT WILL.

IT'S ALL ABOUT DESIRE. YOU JUST GOTTA COME OUT AND DO WHAT YOU GOTTA DO. WE WANTED IT REAL BAD, AND ME AS THE LEADER, I HAD TO COME OUT AND DO MY BEST AND HOPEFULLY THE TEAM COULD RALLY AROUND ME.

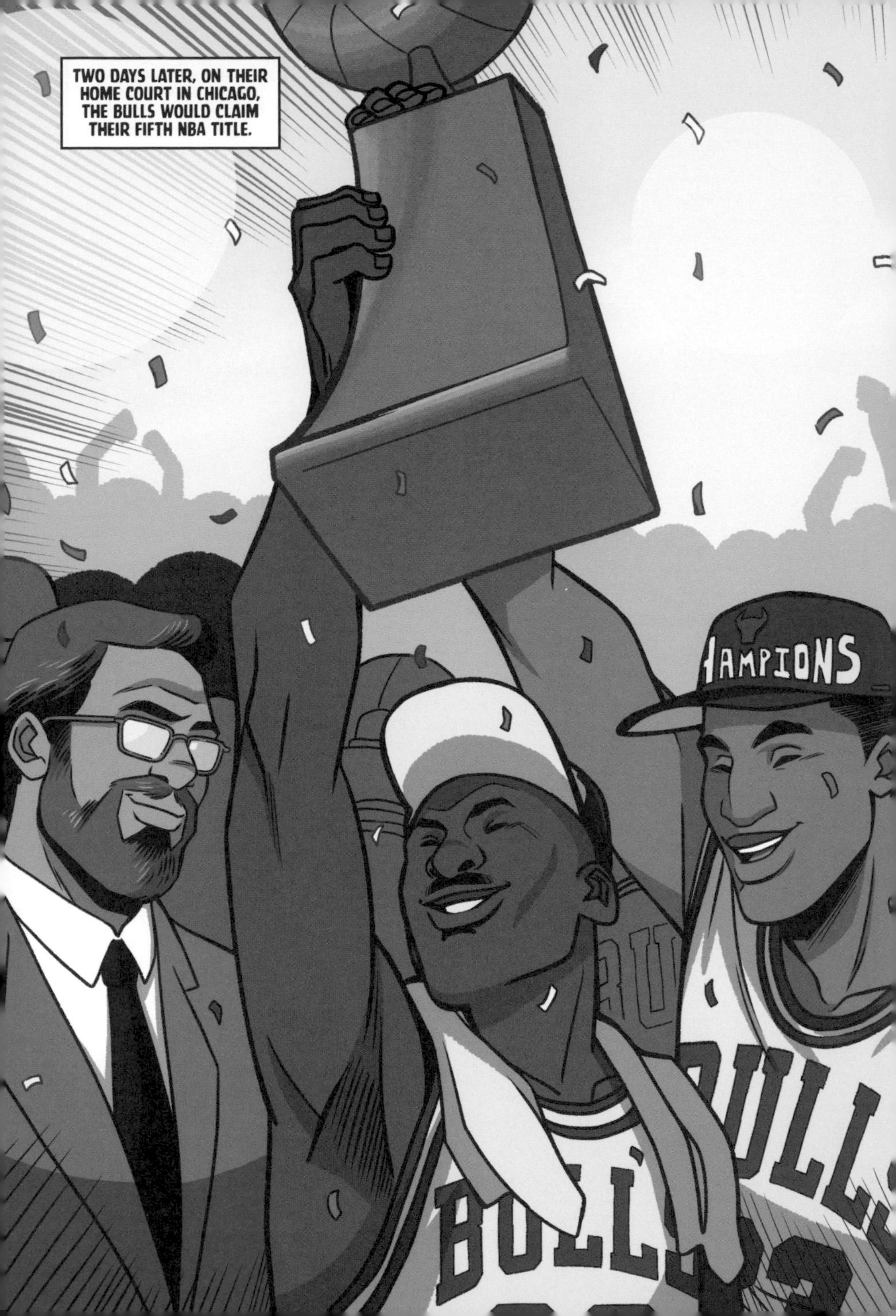
TWO DAYS LATER, ON THEIR HOME COURT IN CHICAGO, THE BULLS WOULD CLAIM THEIR FIFTH NBA TITLE.
HAMPIONS
BULLS

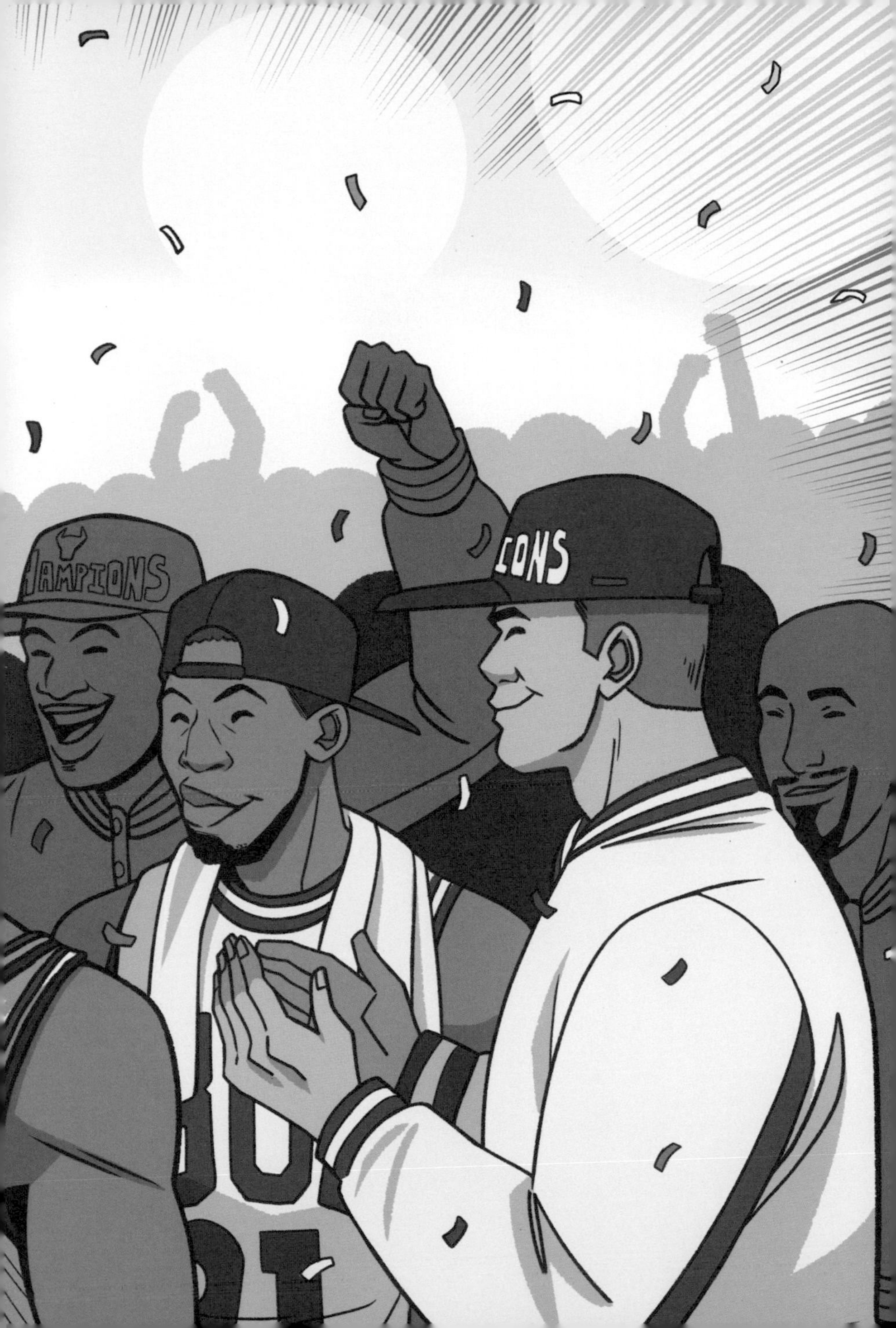
HAMPIONS
ICONS

Conclusion

After winning the fifth game in the 1997 NBA Finals, the Chicago Bulls and Michael Jordan went on to defeat the Utah Jazz in the next championship game on June 12, 1997, on their home court. Jordan would later be named the Most Valuable Player (MVP) of the series. The next year, the Bulls would face the Jazz again at the NBA Finals and would once again emerge victorious. Michael Jordan would win a total of six championship rings in his NBA career.

Jordan retired after that win, his second retirement from basketball. Three years later, he would return to the NBA, but this time to play with the Washington Wizards from 2001 to 2003, after which he retired for the third and final time. Though still a great player, Jordan's seasons with the Wizards never saw him achieve the heights he had with the Bulls. His championship win in 1998 would be his last, and his performance in Game Five of the 1997 NBA series—which would come to be known as "The Flu Game" despite the other theories about the origin of Jordan's sickness—would go down in history as one of the greatest ever played by one of the greatest—if not *the* greatest—basketball players in the sport.

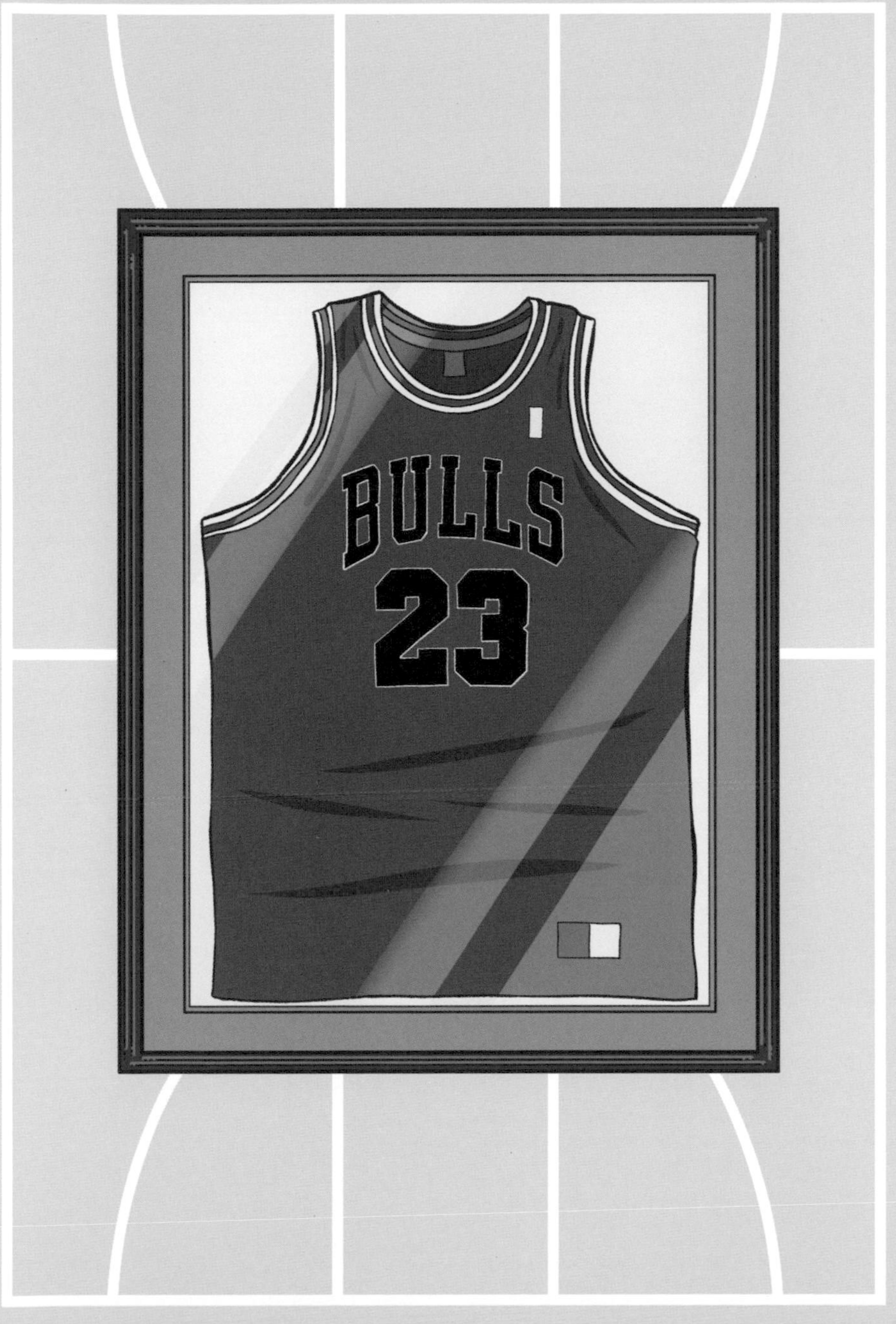
BULLS
23

Timeline of Michael Jordan's Life

1963 — Born in Brooklyn, New York

1978 — Becomes a junior varsity (and later varsity) player on the Emsley A. Laney High School basketball team

1982 — Wins the NCAA basketball championship with the University of North Carolina Tar Heels

1984 — Drafted by the Chicago Bulls

— Wins first Olympic gold medal at the Summer Games in Los Angeles

1991 — Wins first NBA championship with the Bulls

1992 — Wins second NBA championship with the Bulls

— Wins second gold medal as part of the "Dream Team" at the 1992 Olympics in Barcelona

1993 — Wins third NBA championship with the Bulls and retires for the first time

1995 — Rejoins the Bulls

1996 — Wins fourth NBA championship with the Bulls

1997 — Wins fifth NBA championship with the Bulls

1998 — Wins sixth NBA championship with the Bulls and retires for the second time

2003 — Retires from basketball for the third and final time

Bibliography

*Books for young readers

*Anderson, Kirsten. *Who Is Michael Jordan?* New York: Penguin Workshop, 2019.

*Christopher, Matt, with Glenn Stout and Stephanie Peters. *Legends in Sports: Michael Jordan*. New York: Little, Brown and Company, 1996.

Halberstam, David. *Playing for Keeps: Michael Jordan and the World He Made*. New York: Random House, 1999.

Hehir, Jason, dir. *The Last Dance*. 2020. Los Angeles: ESPN Films/Netflix, 2020, streaming.

Jordan, Michael. *Driven from Within*. New York: Atria Books, 2005.

Krugel, Mitchell. *Jordan: The Man, His Words, His Life*. New York: St. Martin's Press, 1994.

Lazenby, Roland. *Michael Jordan: The Life*. New York: Little, Brown and Company, 2014.

*Motin, Adam. *The Legend of Michael Jordan*. Chicago: Triumph Books, 2000.

Pytka, Joe, dir. *Space Jam*. 1996. Burbank: Warner Brothers, 2016, Blu-ray.

Santiago, Wilfred. *Michael Jordan: Bull on Parade*. Seattle: Fantagraphics, 2014.

Smith, Sam. *There Is No Next: NBA Legends on the Legacy of Michael Jordan*. New York: Diversion Publishing, 2014.

ABOUT THE CREATORS

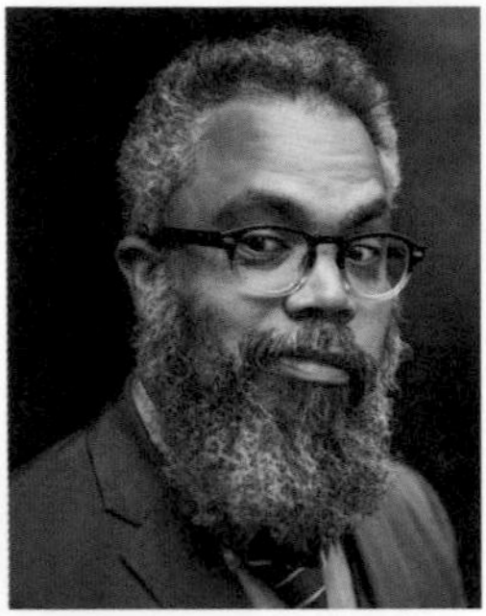

STEVE BURNS

Gabe Soria is best known in the kidlit community for reinventing the choice-driven book genre with his four-book series, Midnight Arcade. He has also written several comic books for DC Comics, including *Batman '66*, and has collaborated with the Black Keys' Dan Auerbach on the *Murder Ballads* comic book.

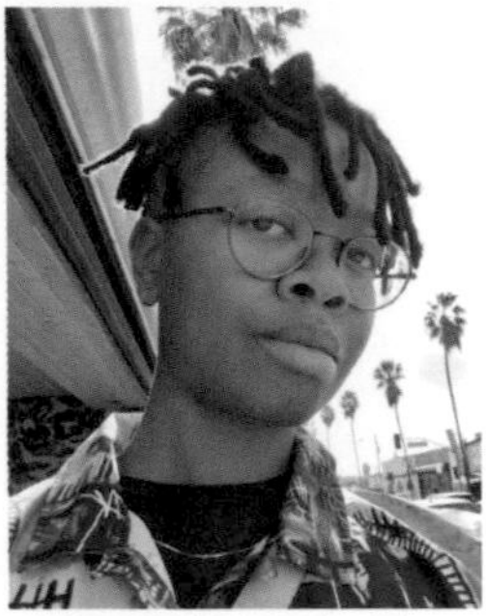

Brittney Williams is a Los Angeles–based creative originally from South Carolina. Williams is a storyboard and comic book artist who draws A LOT. In 2012, she interned at Walt Disney Animation Studios as a storyboard artist. Since then, she's worked for a variety of animation studios and publishers including Netflix, Cartoon Network, DreamWorks TV, BOOM! Studios, DC Comics, and Marvel Comics. As a two-time GLAAD award nominee, she exists to create things for kids and the queer community.